YOU ARE THE LIGHT
OF YOUR CITY

How Christians Can Transform Any City
Through the Power of God

MARK HARRIS

two:twentypress

YOU ARE THE LIGHT OF YOUR CITY
Copyright © 2017 by Mark Harris

All rights reserved. No part of this publication may be reproduced, stored in a retrieval system, or transmitted in any form or by any means – electronic, mechanical, photocopy, recording, or any other – except for brief quotations in printed reviews, without the prior permission of the publisher.

All Scripture quotations, unless otherwise indicated, are taken from the Holy Bible, New King James Version *, Copyright © 1982 by Thomas Nelson, Inc.™ Used by permission. All rights reserved worldwide.

Scripture quotations marked (ESV) are from The Holy Bible, English Standard Version® (ESV®), copyright © 2001 by Crossway, a publishing ministry of Good News Publishers. Used by permission. All rights reserved.

Scripture quotations marked (NIV) are from THE HOLY BIBLE, NEW INTERNATIONAL VERSION®, NIV® Copyright © 1973, 1978, 1984, 2011 by Biblica, Inc.™ Used by permission. All rights reserved worldwide.

Scripture quotations marked (NLT) are taken from the Holy Bible, New Living Translation, copyright © 1996, 2004, 2007 by Tyndale House Foundation. Used by permission of Tyndale House Publishers, Inc., Carol Stream, IL 60188. All rights reserved.

Scripture quotations marked (RSV) are from the Revised Standard Version Bible, copyright © 1946, 1952 and 1971 the Division of Christian Education of the National Council of the Churches of Christ in the United States of America. Used by permission. All rights reserved.

ACKNOWLEDGMENTS

This book is dedicated to Lord and Savior Jesus Christ, without whom transformational power would only be a fantasy.

ENDORSEMENTS

"Mark has always been one of my heroes. The idea that you have to be a big church or a megachurch to change your city is just wrong. I've learned frankly the opposite is true — a smaller church and specifically a group of smaller churches can do more to change and impact a city than a single big church. Mark tells his story and maps out how it all came about. It's not ideas, sermons, and theories—it's the practices that have led them to be able to do what they have. Read it and learn and apply."

Bob Roberts
Sr. Pastor Northwood Church, Keller, Texas
Author most recently of Lessons from the East

"You Are the Light of Your City is a story of inspiration and perspiration. What began as a vision has become a movement that is helping all people of Tucson live and experience life a little closer to the way God intended. In this compact volume, Mark Harris takes us backstage and lets us peek at the nuts and bolts...the structures and relationships that go into the inspired work of city transformation. Filled with strategic insights along with reflective and diagnostic questions, this book serves as a primer for those hearty kingdom-oriented souls who long for what God wants to do in their cities."

Eric Swanson
Leadership Network
Co-author of The Externally Focused Church and To Transform a City

"My friend Mark is a leader and example of someone who truly loves his city, and believes that Jesus wants to transform it. Under his leadership, 4Tucscon encourages Jesus followers to obey their calling to be 'ambassadors' for the Kingdom of God and trust God for biblical transformation that will benefit the whole community. In this compelling book, he reveals a very practical model for how city leaders can approach a long-term transformation effort that begins, first and foremost, with LOVE."

Kevin Palau
President of the Luis Palau Association
Author of "Unlikely- Setting Aside Our Differences to Live Out the Gospel".

TABLE OF CONTENTS

INTRODUCTION
Do You Love Your City?

And seek the peace of the city where I have caused you to be carried away captive, and pray to the LORD for it; for in its peace you will have peace.

Jeremiah 29:7

On a Harley ride with a friend through the southern Rocky Mountains, we stopped to admire the beauty and grandeur of the views all around us. My friend shared, "I just love these mountains. I would live here full time if I could." My thoughts instantly raced to the city where we did live full time— Tucson, Arizona. I asked my friend, Jim Weisert, "Do you love Tucson? Do you love our city like you love these mountains?" Thinking about the question for a moment, he sat back and said, "I don't know that I have ever thought about whether I love Tucson or not. I love the hometown I grew up in, but I don't know that I love Tucson."

The rest of that evening we explored what it meant to love a city. According to the 2010 Census, Tucson is the sixth most impoverished city of similar size in the nation. A few of the questions we discussed that night were:

- Do we grieve for our city because so many people struggle just to make a living?
- Does it bother us when we see graffiti painted on city buildings?
- Do we really care that our schools rank in the bottom 10% of the nation?
- Does it cause us to be sad when we see our city and county governments make foolish decisions about where they spend taxpayer money?

- Does it concern us when people are murdered in the streets overnight?

If you are like most people, answering these types of questions can be depressing. Most Christians falsely believe there is nothing they can do about it, so they just ignore the problems: out of sight, out of mind. When we truly love our cities, we are no more able to block these questions out of our minds than we could ignore a thief bursting through the front door of our house with intent to do our family harm. Do we see the problems of our communities as a real threat to the peace and prosperity of our citizens? Do we love others enough to take responsibility for the problems of our city and allow the blessings of God to flow through us to make their lives better?

City problems that cause people to suffer are the issues Christians are called to address. James 2:15-17 reminds us, *"If a brother or sister is naked and destitute of daily food, and one of you says to them, 'Depart in peace, be warmed and filled,' but you do not give them the things which are needed for the body, what does it profit? Thus also faith by itself, if it does not have works, is dead."*

As Christians in our city, are we guilty of ignoring city problems and saying, in effect, to those who are suffering, *"Peace, be warmed and filled"?*

What can we do? I hope you are asking yourself that question.

This book is about the strategy we are developing in Tucson to fulfill Jesus' command in Matthew 5:16, *"Let your light so shine before men, that they may see your good works and glorify your Father in heaven."* Hopefully, what we have learned so far will help stimulate ideas for how you can demonstrate God's love for your city and the people living in it.

There have been many people over the years who have provided me with critical ideas for developing the city transformational strategy that we now call 4Tucson. I would like to acknowledge that anything I share in this book may have been an idea that originated from another leader or thinker in the country. To the best of my ability, when I can remember where an idea came from, I will give credit. I would also like to take this moment to thank all of the people who have helped shape and influence my thinking about city transformation. Whether or not I understood it at the time that they directly contributed to my development. To those whose ideas I have used, but am unaware, I ask your forgiveness for not acknowledging you. I know nothing misses His gaze, and know that God will bless your involvement in shaping and influencing me.

If God is stirring you to love your city... if God is calling you to change your city by applying biblical principles... and if there is a small group of equally committed Christians willing to take this journey with you, then this book is intended for you. My goal is to pass on our collective knowledge of city transformation to Christian leaders, like you, who are answering God's call to transform your city. May God give you the desires of your heart.

CHAPTER 1
Welcome to the Culture Wars

For we do not wrestle against flesh and blood, but against principalities, against powers,
against the rulers of the darkness of this age, against spiritual hosts of
wickedness in the heavenly places.
Ephesians 6:12

American Christians have been very blessed to live in a country that has traditionally honored religious liberty. In other parts of the world Christians have not been so fortunate. In many countries around the world, Christians are on the frontlines of a war that has been raging since the beginning of time.

Our nation was founded more than 240 years ago by Christians who were fleeing persecution from the enemies of religious freedom in their countries of origin. They came to America to worship freely and eventually established a governmental system that protected that right. Most American Christians in our generation have difficulty grasping the fact we are again in a real war. We are in a battle for our very lives. The bulwark of protection of religious liberty afforded to citizens in our nation's founding documents is rapidly collapsing. We are being overrun by an enemy that wants to take us captive, bind us in the chains of religious intolerance and idolatry and hope that we surrender willfully. We are on the frontlines of a cultural war we are ill-equipped to fight.

The great war is between two powerful rivals who have been adversaries since the creation of man. When God created the world, part of His plan was to put man in charge of His creation. He created each individual to be in a loving relationship with Him and for mankind to rule and reign over His kingdom, with Him as King. God's archenemy tempted man to change allegiances. Sin tempted man to rule and reign over the kingdom of God for his own pleasure rather than for the pleasure of God. From the very minute Adam and Eve switched sides in the great war and were consequentially kicked out of the garden, Satan began a full-scale assault, waging war on God's kingdom. Satan is laying siege to the kingdom of God with the full intent of having dominion over all of God's creation and demanding the worship of his conquered subjects.

The word "kingdom" literally means rule or reign. Jesus said, *"I must preach the kingdom of God to the other cities also, because for this purpose I have been sent" (Luke 4:43)*. The terms *"kingdom of God"* and *"kingdom of heaven"* are used approximately 130 times in the New Testament. Almost all of the parables Jesus taught start with the words, *"The kingdom of God is like..."* Through the parables Jesus explained the nature of the war between these two powerful kingdoms and our personal involvement in that war.

Think what the world would be like today if God had abandoned His authority over His kingdom on earth. What if Satan had been left to his devices and had become the sovereign ruler over God's kingdom? The world would have become a total, living hell. Fortunately for us, God never ceded His power, dominion, or sovereignty over His kingdom. He did not abandon us to the ravages of Satan. His grace has held evil at bay.

The followers of Jesus are engaged in an epic battle for the hearts and souls of mankind. In the interlude between the siege of Satan at the Garden of Eden and the return of Jesus to defeat His ancient foe once and for all, you and I will be engaged in many battles to defend the kingdom of God. In between skirmishes with Satan, Christians are to be on a massive search and rescue mission to liberate the captives who strayed into the enemy's camp and are being held hostage by the power of darkness. *"Or how can one enter a strong man's house and plunder his goods, unless he first binds the strong man? And then he will plunder his house. He who is not with Me is against Me, and he who does not gather with Me scatters abroad" (Matthew 12:29-30).*

Most believers agree we are to proclaim liberty to the captives who have been ensnared and imprisoned by one of Satan's evil schemes. Jesus said, *"The Spirit of the LORD is upon Me, because He has anointed Me to preach the gospel to the poor; He has sent Me to heal the brokenhearted, to proclaim liberty to the captives and recovery of sight to the blind, to set at liberty those who are oppressed" (Luke 4:18).*

There is less agreement found within the Christian community about what the *"kingdom of God"* visibly looks like within a city. Catholics and some Protestants teach the "kingdom of God" is the institutional church. So the phrase "kingdom work" would refer to "church work." Conservative Christians tend to refer to the "kingdom of God" as being in the hearts of individual Christians and they connect the "kingdom" with individually living a spiritual life. The more liberal wing of Christianity associates "kingdom of God" with social reform. Still other Christians believe the "kingdom of God" will be somewhere in the future and will be established during the 1,000-year reign of Jesus on the earth.

My purpose is not to reconcile these diverse views of the kingdom of God. My purpose is to propose that we are all called to be ambassadors for the kingdom of God. An ambassador is an official envoy appointed to be a resident representative of one sovereign government to another sovereign government. You and I are living in this generation to serve as resident ambassadors in our communities, representing the interests of our true King.

This book is about serving our cities as resident representatives of the government of God on earth. We are to help bring the structures and institutions of our cities into alignment with the principles of the kingdom of

God. The more closely our businesses, schools, governments, nonprofits, and churches follow the principles of the kingdom of God, the less people suffer from Satan's cruel siege on humanity.

This book is also about 4Tucson, a model we have been developing that has produced promising results for aligning city structures and institutions with biblical principles. Our desire is to see *"Thy will be done in Tucson, as it is in heaven."* We hope that what we have learned will encourage and challenge you as an ambassador for the kingdom of God in the culture wars of your city.

CHAPTER 2
Are You the Obstacle?

Now as He drew near, He saw the city and wept over it.

Luke 19:41

As part of my seminary training, I read, *Church Planting for a Greater Harvest*, (Ventura, Calif.: Regal Books, 1990) by C. Peter Wagner. In it Wagner said, "Planting new churches is the most effective evangelistic methodology known under heaven."

I believed that then, and still do. Out of seminary, I prayed for an opportunity to go to one of the most unchurched cities in America to begin planting churches. I was blessed to be called by twelve committed Christians to be their pastor for the purpose of planting a local church in their community. They wanted to plant a church in the northeast corner of Tucson, Arizona. While my wife, Debbie, thought trusting twelve people to support our family of five might be a little risky, I couldn't have been more excited. Here was an opportunity to put into practice what I had learned from Wagner's book. According to one study, Tucson was the twelfth most unchurched city our size in the nation. A more recent study by Leadership Network 2014 confirmed that to be still true. Debbie and I accepted the call.

Our new church plant intentionally met in a public school so we could spend our money on planting more churches across the city. Over the next ten years, our little church helped plant 18 churches around Tucson. On my tenth anniversary as pastor at Oasis Church, we conducted a census of all those church plants. Sixteen were still active and growing. Weekly attendance of all the churches combined was more than 3,800 people and more than 1,200 had accepted Christ through one of those churches. The people of Oasis were so gracious to me at my 10-year anniversary celebration. We were overwhelmed by the many lives God had changed through our obedience. Even during the celebration, I could not escape the feeling that something was not right.

- Had we been obedient to what we understood God had called us to do? Yes.
- Were godly pastors leading the church plants? Yes.
- Were individual lives being transformed by the power of God? Yes.
- Was there evidence that the city was improving because individual lives were being transformed? *NO!*

There was the problem. C. Peter Wagner was right that planting churches was a highly effective evangelism method. We had proven that to be true. But somewhere in my mind, I had created the idea that transformed people would result in a transformed city. After a little investigative research, I discovered that after my 10 years as pastor, our city was actually worse off by almost every statistic I could measure. Crime had dramatically increased. Murders and student dropout rates had increased. Divorce and suicide rates were climbing. Bankruptcies were at an all-time high. Drug use was epidemic and a higher percentage of the population of our city had little or no interest in Jesus.

While individual lives were being transformed by the power of Jesus, the power of the kingdom of darkness seemed to advance with little resistance. Why wasn't planting churches transforming our city? Because transforming people is not the same thing as transforming a city. While church planting was the most effective strategy for transforming people, from our experience it seemed that a totally different strategy would need to be developed for effectively transforming a city.

The church I pastored stopped intentionally planting churches after our celebration. We needed to reassess and discover why we had had so little impact on changing our city. I started praying diligently. I continued to faithfully ask God, "How does the power of Your word and the capacity of transformed people change a city? What is the most effective strategy for city transformation?"

Good News and Bad News:
The good news is God answered my prayer.

The bad news is, He told me I was part of the problem. I was taken aback. "God, how could I be part of the problem?" I bristled at the revelation and tried to validate what I had done by asking a few questions of my own.

- Lord, did I not faithfully plant churches as I was taught?
- Lord, have I not demonstrated integrity in my personal life?
- Lord, have I not been instrumental in introducing many people to You through these church plants?
- Lord, have I not done what you asked of me?

"If I have been faithful in those things, how could I be part of the problem? Surely you didn't mean I was part of the problem. I must have misunderstood what You are saying to me. Please clarify what You are saying to me," I prayed.

I never felt God was disappointed in all that I had zealously tried to do for Him. I had, in fact, been obedient to what I understood God had called me to do. Through more prayer, God revealed to me that city transformation would require His whole body, not just one pastor or even one church. For His body to come together in unity was the very prayer Jesus prayed (John 17) just before going to the cross. City transformation would require His whole body working together for a singular purpose. God convicted me that I had not tried to build relationships with other pastors or other churches in the city. I had ignored the other parts of His body in our city. In fact, I arrogantly believed in my heart that many of the pastors in the city were themselves part of the problem. I reasoned that if they were faithful to follow God and worked to see more people come to Christ, our city wouldn't be in the mess it was in. I was doing all I could, why weren't they? It still hurts to admit my arrogance and pride.

For context, I came from the business world before going to seminary and becoming a pastor. Most of the problems businesses face are a direct reflection of the business owner or his/her surrogates. While in business, I often had pastors invite me to lunch, usually to ask for money for their latest building project or mission fund. Some of those meetings were at the root of my negative image of pastors. I would often think in my mind, "It is no wonder our world is in the mess it is in if God entrusted the Gospel to pastors. What was He thinking? Business people could do a lot better job."

God certainly has a sense of humor. About five years into my business career, I felt God calling me into the pastoral ministry. "Are You kidding, God?" I would ask. "You want me to be a pastor!? No way."

One example that caused me to become so jaded toward pastors was they would call me to go to lunch and always expected me to pay the lunch tab. Prior to becoming a pastor, I could not think of a single invitation where that was not true. While pastors talked to me about giving and being generous, they didn't seem to practice what they preached.

With such a negative impression of pastors, surely that tugging in my heart to become a pastor was just indigestion. If I ignored it long enough, I believed, it would eventually go away.

After several years of working in the business world, I started going to seminary once a week. It took seven years; working, going to school, and my wife and I having two babies during that time. I eventually graduated with a

Master's Degree. Yes, after a long spiritual struggle, I agreed to go into pastoral ministry. God always gets His way. After being a modern day Jonah, trying to avoid going into ministry, I finally ended up in my own version of Nineveh — Tucson, Arizona. With a wife and three young kids in tow, we set out to change the world. My youngest daughter was just four weeks old when we rolled into town.

During my times of prayer and reflection on the first 10 years of my ministry, I had come to realize that the problems of the city were not the fault of pastors after all. I had met many really quality men and women serving God with all their hearts. In my first decade of ministry I had not wanted to have anything to do with other pastors and Christian leaders. God was convicting me that my attitude toward those He had called to be pastors was the first problem that had to be remedied if I was going to have the opportunity to participate in any type of city transformation movement. I spent the next 12 months meeting with pastor after pastor, confessing my sinfulness, seeking their forgiveness for having a bad attitude and confessing my jaded spirit toward them. I had to personally ask each of them for forgiveness. I confessed that I had not valued building friendships even when they initiated them and I had little concern for them. I had become a proud, self-centered jerk. I am in awe God still wanted to use me.

More Good News:
Many of the pastors to whom I had gone, and humbled myself, and asked for their forgiveness, were genuinely forgiving and empathetic. They demonstrated a significantly deeper spiritual level of maturity toward me than I had toward them. God showed me in a tangible way just how special many of the pastors in our city really were. Over that 12 months, my jaded view of pastors melted away. God has now given me a real respect for the call He has placed on people in ministry. He has given me genuine concern for pastors, ministry leaders, and their families. He has given me a heart of compassion for the hardships they endure and the sacrifices they make to advance the

kingdom of God. I now genuinely pray for their provision and success.

It was a difficult year of God continually bringing to mind one pastor after another to whom I needed to humble myself and ask for forgiveness. As I was obedient to meet with those pastors, God also began to reveal a strategy for mobilizing and engaging Christians for genuine city transformation. I believe it was only after my obedience that God revealed the strategy for city transformation.

This book is about that strategy.

If you are sincere about changing your city for the glory of God, I would strongly suggest you start with an extended time in prayer before attempting to implement this strategy. Let God examine your heart and reveal any areas that are not consistent with leading a city movement. Follow through in obedience with what He shows you. If you shortcut this process, I am convinced you will not have the character to endure what it takes to change your city. Many Christian leaders start out strong, only to yield to a character flaw that eventually blows them up — usually in a public way. You do not want to be that person. Instead, be the leader that goes the distance. You will need time with God to work through any of those issues before you enter enemy territory.

Honestly search your heart before God. Find answers to questions like the ones below to help assess where you are in your personal preparation process. Don't be afraid to ask the hard questions:

- Am I at a place spiritually where God can use me to lead others in a city transformation movement?
- Do I have the character to lead a city transformation?
- Do I have the emotional stability to endure the high highs and low lows of city transformation?

I am sincere in my caution: **do not start a city transformation effort until**

you are spiritually ready. You also need to understand the importance of not trying this alone. You will need other mature believers to take the journey with you. An African proverb is a good reminder of that: "If you want to go fast, go alone. If you want to go far, go together."

I have learned from my own experience it is not wise to attempt to do great things for God if your heart is not prepared for the task ahead. Our enemy does not give up dominion without a fight. You had better be spiritually, emotionally, and mentally ready for the fight. You will also need a committed team to do the work with you. If you take city transformation seriously, it is easy to feel fearful and overwhelmed. I challenge you to have a healthy respect for what is ahead, prepare as best you can, but don't let fear or the size of the task paralyze you. There must come a time where you commit to get into the fight or nothing in your city will change.

Examine me, O LORD, and prove me; Try my mind and my heart.
Psalm 26:2

CHAPTER 3
Personal Transformation Does Not Equal City Transformation

Also, seek the peace and prosperity of the city to which I have carried you into exile.
Pray to the LORD for it, because if it prospers, you too will prosper.
Jeremiah 29:7 (NIV)

Why would Christians want to transform a city? Tim Keller, former pastor of Redeemer Presbyterian Church in Manhattan, New York, said, "As more and more people become city-dwellers, it is imperative that the church understands how to reach out to the expanding cities of the 21st century. God designed the city with the power to draw out the resources of creation (of the natural order and the human soul) and thus to build civilization."

The Holy Spirit seems to be moving across America and in other places in the world with the same message for Christians: Engage your community. It is not a new message. We have always been called to be salt and light in our world. It has only been within the last few years that Christians in America have reawakened to the idea that the very cities in which we live are in desperate need of an infusion of the blessings of God. Other than a vacation, traveling to another city for business or maybe a mission trip, few of us venture too far from home. That ought to make it even more of a priority for us to make the city where we live one of the best places in the world to live. Desiring the peace and prosperity of our city and praying specifically for it ought to be a priority.

It doesn't take but one glance at the headlines of a local newspaper to become dazed with the magnitude of city problems. The problems of your city may not be your fault, but as ambassadors for the kingdom of God, they are your responsibility. If you agree, then the first question becomes, "How do we as Christians fix the problems that hurt people and keep them in bondage?" The next question is, "What strategy should we employ to do something about the problems we see?"

For the benefit of developing common language, we are calling the process of Christians fixing city problems "City Transformation." City Transformation happens as Christians bring city structures and institutions into alignment with biblical principles.

My first encounter with other Christians who were not just thinking about city transformation but were actually experimenting with functional models was when I was invited to attend a Glocalnet Conference in Dallas, Texas with Bob Roberts. Bob is the Pastor of Northwood Baptist Church. At that meeting he challenged us to answer two questions: 1) What would happen if the church became the missionary in your city? 2) When will Jesus be enough for you? Bob has written several books that will challenge you and help you explore both of those questions in greater detail. For the purpose of this book, suffice it to say those questions challenged me. They fueled my quest to find the answers to why church planting alone did not transform my city.

Bob's model at that time was to mobilize his entire church to become the missionary to Vietnam. His idea was to use the expertise of the members of his church to help transform circles of influence in another nation. Those circles of influence were called Domains of Society. An example of a domain in action was education. Teachers and administrators within the Education Domain would work with teachers and administrators in the same domain in Vietnam. His church enjoyed great success and saw remarkable transformation in the education system of that country.

A few years later at another event Bob invited me to, I met Eric Swanson. He had just co-authored a book with Rick Rusaw called, *"The Externally Focused Church."* That book challenged the church to work outside its four walls and to creatively engage the culture around them. What should have been obvious from the Scripture did not seem to be obvious to most of us in attendance. The problems in our cities were there because Christians, by and large, were absent from the public square. Swanson and Rusaw proposed new ways for the church to fulfill its mandate. They challenged churches to think about how the needs and dreams of the city directly intersect the mandates of God and how those two intersect the calling and sending capacity of the church. Where those three circles intersect was what Swanson called the "sweet spot." The sweet spot was service. Serving others is where Christians have the most opportunity for city engagement. This is the diagram Swanson used to illustrate his idea.

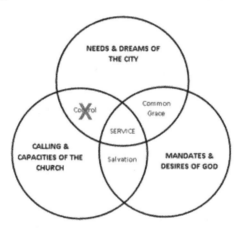

And he sat down and called the twelve. And he said to them, "If anyone would be first, he must be last of all and servant of all." Mark 9:35

Swanson pointed out, that most of the time, the struggle between the city and the church was around the issue of control. Christians have the reputation of being adversarial toward city leaders who are trying to achieve the needs and dreams of the city. Swanson advocated that when Christians approach the city with a heart of service, we will find many doors are open that were previously closed.

Most Christians would agree that the Bible has the answers for the most difficult problems individuals face. By applying biblical principles in their personal lives, individuals can be radically transformed by the power of God and they are then able to enjoy the bounty of God's blessings. *"And do not be conformed to this world, but be transformed by the renewing of your mind, that you may prove what is that good and acceptable and perfect will of God"* (Romans 12:2).

By expanding our biblical paradigm of transformation to include the church being the missionary to the city, service becomes the key that opens doors of opportunity. Reading the Bible using that paradigm, we started to see the Word of God reveal principles for radically transforming the most difficult and systemic problems of a city. It is a statement of fact that city transformation will not happen without biblically transformed people. That is why evangelism and planting churches must be a part of any city transformation strategy. People whose lives have been transformed by the grace of Jesus begin to develop a different worldview as their minds are transformed by the Scriptures. The people who are not yet Jesus followers have minds that conform to the world. Those who are not Jesus followers will continue to make decisions based on the destructive worldview of the kingdom of Satan. They do not, nor can they, share the same worldview as those of us who are resident representatives of the kingdom of God.

Competing worldviews is what sets the stage for a potential clash over control in a city. The problems in every city are, in most cases, the result of leaders who apply ideologies and philosophies in decision-making that are contrary to the Bible. As well-intentioned as they might be, their worldview causes them to make harmful, even destructive choices for citizens. Their lack of understanding of the ways of God actually creates more problems or leads to unintended consequences while they are trying to solve a specific problem facing the city.

The unintended consequences continue to build in a city until something eventually breaks — economic collapse, cultural collapse, even revolution in some cases. Many of the problems that cause severe stress on a community can be traced to policy decisions or laws that are enacted that do not align with biblical principles. These decisions are made by leaders whose hearts are not aligned with Jesus. When Christians in America see these things happening, and if they disagree strongly enough, they may show up at a city council meeting to voice their displeasure. Christians have little impact on the policy using that strategy. They then drift back into their daily routine and discuss with their Christian friends how the world is going to hell in a handbasket and how Christians have little influence in society. From experiences like these, we often draw a false conclusion that Christians and our views are not welcome in the public square. However, it is not our message that is the problem. It is our strategy.

The unintended, adverse consequences of policies passed by leaders who do not understand biblical principles can be seen in most cities around the United States. As Christians, we should not expect to have any meaningful impact on the policies or laws passed by our elected leaders by simply showing up once a year to a city council meeting with a grievance. Frustrated, some Christians get involved in another tactic to make needed change. They invest money in supporting candidates for elected office who more closely reflect their personal worldview. But replacing elected leaders who do not share a biblical worldview with new leaders who do, has proven to be a disappointing strategy. The reason the newly elected officials are not successful is because they are unable to change the structures and institutions that, by design, are in place to protect the culture from radical changes.

Structures and institutions, by design, are slow to change and because they are slow to change they provide cultural stability. When a city or nation has structures and institutions that have been entrenched for long periods of time, bureaucracies form around them that further resist change. Electing a different politician, even a Christian politician, who must work within the bureaucratic structures and institutions cannot, by the very nature of the system, make many effective changes.

Sustainable city transformation starts with an honest look at the most difficult problems within a city. Christians must do research on the policies, structures and institutions that perpetuate city problems. The questions that Christians should ask are:

- How did we get here?
- Is the problem an unintended consequence of trying to solve a different problem?
- What are the structural and institutional changes that need to be made to fix the problem?
- Who are the key people in the city who are directly responsible for guarding the status quo?

Hopefully, by answering these types of questions, it will become clear that city transformation will take a strategy that is fundamentally different from the one used for individual transformation. While it is true biblical city transformation will not happen without God honoring, transformed people, transformed people alone are not enough. Biblical city transformation requires Christians to apply biblical principles at a macro level, dealing with the city as a whole, while also focusing at a micro level, dealing with people as individuals. We must learn to think differently about the city and its people. It is not one strategy verses the other, it is both at the same time. An effective city transformation strategy will deal with the problems of the city and the problems of the individual but each in different ways.

CHAPTER 4
What Is Biblical City Transformation and Why Is It Important?

You are the light of the world. A city that is set on a hill cannot be hidden.
Matthew 5:14

Many people use the term "City Transformation," but few can define it. 4Tucson's working definition of Biblical City Transformation is bringing all of the city structures and institutions into alignment with biblical principles to help the largest number of people possible. God invented the city. The word "city" is used more than 850 times in the Bible. The city is a center of population, commerce, and culture of significant size and importance when compared to the surrounding geographical area. God's purpose for the city is to provide a place where people collectively utilize the resources of creation to build civilization. Psalm 107 is particularly insightful when looking at a city that follows the ways of God verses a city that does not.

Before Biblical City Transformation is possible, it is helpful to have a working definition of the term "city." What constitutes a city is surprisingly subjective. What a city actually is, where it begins and ends, and who has governing authority over specific geographical areas are all matters of debate. Any attempt at specificity will likely only create many inconsistencies. Because the definition of city is vague, the key when talking about city transformation is to keep a keen eye on your working definition of "city." For those of us working in Tucson, the term "city" includes a geographical metro-area that encompasses several municipalities. Several of those municipalities would argue they are completely autonomous and are not part of the city of Tucson. There is not an easy solution to defining our city. You may find the same problem in your city. But you will need a working definition if you are going to begin the process of biblical change.

When talking about transforming our city, the word "transformation" by most definitions involves a thorough or dramatic change in form and function. At 4Tucson, we make a distinction between transformation and biblical transformation. Most people, when they envision city transformation, think of positive change. However, there is such a thing as malignant transformation. When a physical body experiences malignant transformation, it is usually some form of cancer. That type of transformation, at worst, kills the host; at best it causes stress and diminished function. A typical city will have many malignancies — negative transformations that are not positive, that cause people harm, maybe even death. Institutionalized abortion would be an example of negative transformation.

Biblical Transformation, as defined by 4Tucson, is a restoration to the original purpose and intent of God. This will be a paradigm shift for many leaders. It bears repeating that Biblical City Transformation is bringing the city structures and institutions into alignment with biblical principles for the benefit of the largest number of people possible. We can change the names of the mayor or city council every election cycle, but unless we address the cultural problems at a structural and institutional level, transformation will be dramatically slow or non-existent and, in some cases, malignant.

In a city context, biblical transformation is a process of profound and radical change that orients the city's structures and institutions to align with biblical principles. The closer a city gets to that ideal, the more the city will receive a new level of blessing and success. When the city moves in the direction of biblical alignment, the city will experience a greater level of policy effectiveness and the citizens will receive the benefits of God's blessings and common grace.

Unlike "turnaround," which implies incremental progress on the same plane, transformation implies a basic change of character and little or no resemblance with the past configuration or structure. A couple of questions we hear from time to time are:

- Why should Christians be interested in City Transformation?
- Shouldn't we just focus on evangelism? (individual transformation)

My question in return to those who ask is, "As ambassadors of the kingdom of God, is there any part of our city that we are willing to surrender to the kingdom of Satan?"

If I understand Daniel 7:27 correctly, then you and I have been given authority by God to bring our cities under the dominion of Christ: *"Then the kingdom and dominion, and the greatness of the kingdoms under the whole heaven, shall be given to the people, the saints of the Most High. His kingdom is an everlasting kingdom, and all dominions shall serve and obey Him."*

We are to love people like Jesus commanded us. Cities, by whatever definition is used, are where large numbers of those people live. When people within a particular city suffer, Christians should care. Cities are a direct reflection of the worldview of the people who live in them. To experience the blessings of God, the structures and institutions of the city must align with what God can bless.

Isn't that the message of Jonah? Nineveh was a wicked, corrupt city. Jonah believed that the city was in need of judgment, not redemption. When Jonah shared God's message, the entire city repented and turned to God. In Jonah 3:6-10, the king, who was sovereign, by edict determined the structures and institutions of Nineveh need to be changed to align with what he understood God to declare. In our cities it will take more than an edict.

The angst many Christians have toward their cities opens them up to be tempted by the great Deceiver. They often pray for and seek the judgment of God rather than His mercy. Because the citizens of Nineveh had rejected God and His principles, Jonah was actually angry at God for showing mercy and transforming Nineveh when the citizens repented. It displeased Jonah exceedingly, and he became fuming mad. So he prayed to the LORD, and said, *"Ah, LORD, was not this what I said when I was still in my country? Therefore, I fled previously to Tarshish; for I know that You are a gracious and merciful God, slow to anger and abundant in lovingkindness, One who relents from doing harm"* (Jonah 4:1-2).

Throughout the Bible, most easily identifiable in the books of Judges or 1 Samuel, we see that the collective actions of one city can cause it to prosper, while the collective actions of another city can cause it distress and crisis. Today, we see the same pattern and the same results from both good and bad city decisions being played out across the urban landscape of America. Every city makes decisions in their own unique way, usually through some form of representative governance, leaving time to reveal whether the decisions of those in authority were wise and beneficial, or foolish and harmful. Wise decisions tend to resolve problems and promote city-wide prosperity. Poor decisions usually result in needless suffering spread over an entire population of a city.

It is obviously preferable for a city to make wise decisions rather than try to fix the problems created by poor decisions. So for biblical city transformation to be effective, Christians must look for opportunities to shape and influence current city decisions. At the same time, they need to be working to discover and implement biblical solutions to the complex problems that no one in authority knows how to fix.

From where does the wisdom for making wise decisions that benefit the citizens come? Proverbs 9:10 says, *"The fear of the LORD is the beginning of wisdom, and the knowledge of the Holy One is understanding.*" Here we get our first glimpse of the culture wars in most cities. The God of the Bible is the source of all wisdom.

Proverbs 1:22 says, *"...how long will scoffers delight in their scoffing and fools hate knowledge?"* When those in authority make decisions that mock God, the city will ultimately suffer for it. As mentioned earlier, there are two competing worldviews at the root of all decision making in a city. The competing worldviews are foundational for how every decision is made in a city. Those who are in places of authority to make decisions for a whole city may choose to base their decision-making process on the wisdom and knowledge that God gives through the Bible. That is our preference as Jesus followers. Or, they may choose a worldview that ridicules and mocks God and instead make decisions from a plurality of what the population says is preferred at the time. The consequences for both wise and foolish decisions are felt by the entire community for years. The battles over differing worldviews can be intense. Christians, as a whole, have not demonstrated that they have the stomach for it. It is easier to retreat to their churches and pray for the judgement of God to come on a city that rejects His ways.

As we have researched the problems in Tucson, we have found that good decisions are often discounted over time because they actually solved the problems they were intended to solve. Once a problem is solved, it is out of sight and out of mind. Little reflection is afforded to the source of the wisdom used to make the beneficial decision or whether it aligned with the principles of God.

With the advantage of hindsight, evaluating decisions over time, most citizens would agree that our city — Tucson — is not characterized as a city with a history of making wise decisions. It is very recognizable at election time, where political signs on every street corner highlight one of the city problems. Candidates promise voters that if elected, they are the ones who can fix the problems. Most of the significant problems our city currently faces are the culmination of years of poor decisions and their unintended consequences. As our city grows, the complexity of our problems expose the ill-fated decisions of the past. Entire bureaucracies are built around carrying out those policy decisions and protecting them from change. The consequences of ill-fated decisions only get worse without an intentional transformational process. Politicians, even Christian politicians, may be able to make small changes, but true city transformation requires a different strategy.

Romans 12:2 says, *"Do not conform to the pattern of this world, but be transformed by the renewing of your mind. Then you will be able to test and approve what God's will is—his good, pleasing and perfect will."*

City Transformation starts in earnest when it is realized that the worldview used by those in authority for making decisions directly impacts the entire citizenry. As Christians, we see the value of our leaders intentionally making decisions using the principles of God. They have been proven to work. Throughout history we can observe the results of leaders who did not value biblical wisdom and, therefore, made decisions based on the latest fad or philosophy of the culture. They have been proven not to work. It is discovered too late that those decisions actually caused many people to suffer.

In Tucson, some of our leaders are open to knowing what the Bible says about solving certain city-wide problems. Politicians don't want to appear foolish in the eyes of their constituency. If they don't go to church or read their Bibles regularly, they simply don't know who to ask about what the Bible says. Christians showing up to protest a decision at a city council meeting once every year or so will not help city leaders understand where they are violating a biblical principle nor attract them toward Christians.

There are a handful of leaders in our city that do not share our enthusiasm for using a biblical worldview. Tucson is the 12th most unchurched city in

America. *(Leadership Network, 2014)* Only about 7% of our citizens attend church regularly. It is easy to understand the reluctance of a city leader to trust the Bible for answers when a majority of the citizens sees the world exactly as they do. Leaders, particularly politicians, want their views to be aligned with the majority view of voting citizens. Since the majority of the citizens do not seek biblical wisdom to direct their decisions, the majority of our leaders do not either. Seeking wisdom of the Bible to guide their decisions is out of step with the mainstream of our city. We feel the heaviness of that daily.

As we have worked with our city leaders, it is my observation they genuinely desire to make decisions that benefit the whole community. They rely on their peers or the majority view of the untransformed citizens to make their decisions. Once a policy decision is made, they sit back and hope for the best. When the decision doesn't resolve the problem as they had originally hoped, they feel vindicated by saying, "Well, we at least tried."

What if it was standard operating procedure for our leaders to apply James 1:5 when making decisions? *"If any of you lacks wisdom, let him ask of God, who gives to all liberally and without reproach, and it will be given to him."*

- What if your city leaders had working relationships with godly Christians whom they trusted to ask for biblical counsel about the decisions they are pondering?
- Have you been in the office of your city's mayor to discuss policy?
- Do you personally know the people serving on your city council?
- Do you regularly pray for your city leaders by name?

Asking these types of questions, building city-wide relationships, and praying for those in authority over you are all keys for the transformation of your city.

CHAPTER 5

What Are the Structures and Institutions of a City?

Woe to those who call evil good, and good evil;
Who put darkness for light, and light for darkness;
Who put bitter for sweet, and sweet for bitter!
Isaiah 5:20

The definition of Biblical City Transformation used by 4Tucson is, "To bring the structures and institutions of our city into alignment with biblical principles for the peace and prosperity of the citizens." When a city follows biblical principles, God *"makes His sun rise on the evil and on the good, and sends rain on the just and on the unjust"* (Matthew 5:45).

We recognize the fact that many people and ministries use the term "City Transformation" and that their use of the term may vary depending on the context in which they use it. We found it helpful for our purposes to move away from a contextual definition of city transformation to a more specific definition.

We also recognize that there are additional complex definitions for city structures and institutions. For the purpose of 4Tucson's City Transformation Strategy, we define city ***structures*** as the framework of the city set by its laws and policies which provide form and stability for what is deemed moral and normative behavior of its citizens. Structures will vary from city to city. Some city structures can be accommodating and promote the well-being of its citizens, while other structures can be problematic and oppressive. Examples of structures would include things like speed limits, zoning laws, taxes and business regulations.

We define city *institutions* as those stable, virtuous parts of a culture that define values, customs, and traditions. Institutions serve as cultural guardians that preserve what is deemed to be ethically right and proper from generation to generation necessary for the survival of that culture. Examples of city institutions would include the institution of marriage, the institution of family, the institution of religion, the institution of education, the institution of government.

Conflicts within a city can arise when a majority of citizens deem a particular behavior as moral and the structures and institutions declare that same behavior as immoral. The city structures can be altered by policy decisions and/or changes in law when a majority of citizens believe a particular behavior should be normative going forward. When laws are changed, those laws dictate future citizen behavior and establish the new normal within that culture.

Institutions, on the other hand, have centuries and in some cases, millenniums, of history that support maintaining the timeless values, customs, and traditions that have preserved the civilization during a long period of time. Institutions do not typically change quickly and, therefore, protect the culture from whims and fads that come and go with each generation.

Structures deal with the reality of what "*is*" and *institutions* deal with the ideal of what "*ought to be.*"

Understanding the structures and institutions of a city is important for the purpose of city transformation. It is through the process of aligning these structures and institutions with biblical principles that actually produces sustainable city transformation. Attempting to implement a city transformation process that addresses specific problems but does not address the structures and institutions will only have the effect of a temporary solution. As soon as a change agent moves on to solve the next problem, the original problem gradually returns to its original condition. It is the principle of entropy on a city level. Without intentional change, the systems of laws, policies, and bureaucracies of the city will revert back to the original design that contributed to the problem. People make their living guarding and protecting the status quo. They actually perpetuate the problem, while claiming to want to fix it.

The closer the structures and institutions of a city align with biblical principles, the more opportunity is afforded regular citizens to use all their gifts, talents, and abilities to become what God created them to be. Evil loses its grip on the community — people are safe and families prosper. When structures and institutions don't align biblically, they oppress, crush, and destroy the original design of God for human beings. As evil accelerates, people suffer.

Understanding the structures and institutions of the city are important in another way. When people are allowed to function within a city that more closely aligns with biblical principles, they are more likely to succeed in what God has called them to do. By removing burdensome structures, businesses are more profitable and employ more people. Nonprofits are more effective in delivering services to the "least of these" in the city without bureaucratic red tape.

Misaligned structures and institutions will impede and restrain citizens from receiving the abundance of the blessing of God, which is intended to flow through to the entire community. Misaligned structures and institutions create additional layers of bureaucracy and oppressive rules that cause needless harm, frustration, and stress in the lives of people, while claiming it is for their own good.

At 4Tucson, our model is built around the premise that God wants to use His followers to bring His wisdom into the decision-making processes of every school board, city council, state, and national government. God wants to display His wisdom and power in our communities. He wants to use ordinary Jesus followers to lead the way, providing the conduit for His blessings to flow. *"For it is the God who commanded light to shine out of darkness, who has shone in our hearts to give the light of the knowledge of the glory of God in the face of Jesus Christ. But we have this treasure in earthen vessels, that the excellence of the power may be of God and not of us. We are hard-pressed on every side, yet not crushed; we are perplexed, but not in despair; persecuted, but not forsaken; struck down, but not destroyed"* (2 Corinthians 4:6-9).

Christians are just ordinary people who God will use to confound the foolish and arrogant. Do you remember what the leaders in Jerusalem said about the disciples? *"Now when they saw the boldness of Peter and John, and perceived that they were uneducated and untrained men, they marveled. And they realized that they had been with Jesus"* (Acts 4:13).

We don't expect our citizens or our leaders to immediately start making decisions according to biblical principles. However, we do expect Christians to be engaged in bringing the wisdom of the kingdom of God into the decision-making process by looking for opportunities to serve our city where doors are open. Serving leads to relationships where biblical principles can be shared in conversations without fear of condemnation.

When we have those conversations with city leaders about the 4Tucson Strategy, we say it this way: 4Tucson's strategy is to address our city's most difficult and systemic problems by uniting Christians to envision and implement biblical solutions for the benefit of the whole city.

We explain that we want to help our leaders be successful. We want to provide the opportunity for them to hear what the Bible says about a particular problem. We say, "We pray that God will give you wisdom to make decisions that will benefit the entire city with the least amount of unintended consequences."

Here are some preliminary questions that may help you begin to understand the structures and institutions of your city. They will help you understand the needs and dreams of your city and to identify its decision-making processes. Without answers to these types of questions, you will have little success in sustaining Biblical City Transformation.

1. When was your city established?
2. How large is the city? What is the area and population?
3. What are the structures that determine behavior norms in your city?
4. What are the most influential institutions of your city?
5. What is the unique cultural identity of your city?
6. What major topological features intersect your city?
7. Was your city conceived as a city or did it grow up from a town?
   a. If it grew up from a town, do you have an "old city" district?
   b. Are there other indicators of the old?
   c. Does your city have your city core located somewhere in that old city? What is the relationship between the old and the new parts of the city?
8. What are the unique "hooks" and positive characteristics of your city?
   a. Culture, Entertainment, Sports and Tourism?
   b. Higher Education, Trade, Banking and Manufacturing?
   c. Religious Activity?
9. Have there been attempts at urban renewal?
   a, Identify major projects to protect or replenish different parts of your city.
   b. Identify the urban renewal projects of your city and look for a shift in where populations live and do business.

10. During what technological age was your city built?

a. Was your city built prior to cars and does it tend to have small streets? Pedestrian and bike ways?

b. Was your city built around a railroad or freeway?

c. Was your city built around geographical features that are unique to the area? Are those geographical features viewed as an asset or a liability?

11. What city infrastructure is available in your city?

12. What is the age of the technology of your city?

13. What major industries operate in your city?

a. Do they have their own "districts"?

b. Do they have any topographical needs?

c. What services do they need to be near to be successful? For example: Labor, transportation, storage, warehouses, residential.

14. What is the social stratification in your city?

a. Do the rich loathe the poor?

b. Do the rich take pity on the poor?

c. How many classes or tiers are there in your society?

d. Do the rich and poor mingle or do they avoid one another?

e. Are there orphanages? Slums? Places where each class does not, or cannot go?

15. What is the racial stratification in your city?

a. Is there an effort to intentionally bring people of different ethnic and racial backgrounds together?

b. Are immigrant populations mainstreamed or isolated?

c. Does the city have racially identifiable neighborhoods? Little Italy (Italian), Harlem, Spanish Harlem, Chinatown, etc?

16. Are there any major ceremonies, festivals, religious, or military celebrations that incorporate most or almost all segments of the population?

17. Are there any major roads, highways, or freeways running nearby or through your city?

18. What specialized economic activities or industries are valued in the city?
    a. What are those activities or industries specifically?
    b. Do those industries enjoy special benefits of the citizens and government officials?
19. What is the median income in your city?
20. What percent of the population owns a home?
21. What is the percentage of the population at each educational attainment level?
22. Has your city created strategic plans, blueprints, or other documents that were intended to provide direction for the city?
    a. Do you have access to them? (they should be public)
    b. How many are there?
    c. Who produced them?
    d. How were they received by the community at large?
    e. Were they successful in producing the stated outcome?
23. Does your city government have an organizational chart?
24. How many of the people in the organizational chart do you know or have contact with?
25. Do you know the hopes and dreams they have for the city?
26. Do you know if any of them are Christians? How do you evaluate if they are or are not?
27. Which city leaders would be supportive of Christianity and applying biblical principles to decision making?
28. Which city leaders would be opposed to Christianity and applying biblical principles to decision making?

CHAPTER 6
Start With the End in Mind

There are many plans in a man's heart,
nevertheless, the LORD's counsel – that will stand.
Proverbs 19:21

Up to this point, we have shared our philosophy of Biblical City Transformation in Tucson. I am confident that God is already at work filling your mind with ways you could do the same types of things in your city. There is no "one way" to transform a city. The rest of this book is how we structured the 4Tucson model. I want to give you some reasons why we did it the way we did. Hopefully, our experiences will serve to cut your learning curve substantially. Please feel free to use anything we have learned or developed at 4Tucson. We hope you will share with us what you are doing in your city so we can learn from you, too.

People have often asked me, "What will City Transformation look like when we are finished?" Our working definition of **City Transformation is to bring all of the city structures and institutions into alignment with biblical principles for the peace and prosperity of its citizens.** By that definition, city transformation will never be finished. We live in an imperfect world where humans are always messing things up. We will always be in the process of aligning and re-aligning our city structures and institutions with biblical principles. It takes vigilance and hard work to continually improve the cities we live in. Like a garden, when maintained, it produces fruit. When it is ignored, the land naturally reverts to what it was originally—usually weeds.

Before we go much further, I would like to dispel any notion that city transformation is an easy process. Working with people, ideas, information, strategies, and tactics can be daunting. The biggest challenge we faced and continue to face at 4Tucson is not letting the obstacles and difficult challenges rob us of the joy of loving God, loving each other and loving the people in our city.

We are continually reminded by one of our Domain Directors the importance of honoring one another, laughing, and celebrating with one another at our weekly staff meetings. It has lifted our spirits and built an internal pressure relief system that has helped us endure some of the more difficult times of working in the city. Learn from us. Right from the beginning of your work in the city, incorporate the principle of having fun, laughing together, and praying together along the journey. It is important! If you don't do it intentionally, city transformation will grind you and your team to a pulp. You will need to find the balance between accomplishing the task at hand and building relationships. For most leaders, there will always be tension between getting things done and spending time with people.

One day, while contemplating the question of what city transformation would look like when it was finished, I read Psalm 144. Praying through the Psalm, I realized that it explained what city transformation looked like to God and what we should strive for. Here are some of my personal thoughts on each verse of Psalm 144, and how it has encouraged me to move forward toward our mission. It has become my prayer for city transformation.

Psalm 144
1 A Psalm of David. Blessed be the LORD my Rock, and who trains my hands for war and my fingers for battle.

>   Lord, if we are going to attempt anything great for the kingdom
>   of God in our generation, it will not happen apart from You

revealing Your plans and training us for the challenges ahead. City Transformation is not for the faint of heart. It is hard work. At times it seems like war when dealing with people of influence who do not share our biblical worldview. They don't always understand or see the consequences of their poor decisions. No matter how well- intended, their decisions can have a lasting negative impact on the people of our city. You call us to be ambassadors of Your kingdom and to defend people from those who intentionally or unintentionally do them harm.

2 My loving kindness and my fortress, my high tower and my deliverer, my shield and the One in whom I take refuge, who subdues my people under me.

Lord, it is overwhelming when we stop to consider the opposition from people, organizations, and even government agencies who will challenge the process of implementing Your plans; plans that will benefit the entire city. Many of our fiercest critics are those who have a vested interest in the status quo. They make their paycheck each month by being guardians of the structures and institutions of the city. They will defend their positions fervently.

We rest confidently in the love You have for us. We trust that it is You who will be our Refuge and Deliverer when the fiery darts of the enemy are aimed directly at us. We will subdue those in opposition by trusting in Your promises and Your shield.

3 LORD, what is man, that You take knowledge of him? Or the son of man, that You are mindful of him?

We are the apple of Your eye. We are Your delight. We are the pinnacle of Your creation. In Your amazing way, You are able to pay attention to all of us, at all times, in all ways. We are very grateful that You allow us to participate in Your kingdom plans, and we also marvel in Your confidence in us as Your ambassadors to our city.

4 Man is like a breath; His days are like a passing shadow.

> The days of our lives on earth are finite. In the blink of an eye they are over. They go by quickly. Each day is a gift from You and must be used wisely. Help us make the most of every opportunity. Help us to wisely walk through every open door while we have breath.

5 Bow down Your heavens, O LORD, and come down; Touch the mountains, and they shall smoke.

> When the citizens of our city see Your power in tangible ways, when they see Your power as obvious and as clear as smoke on a mountain, then they will yield to Your plans and purposes. Seeing Your presence emboldens us and gives us courage to continue to move forward in the face of opposition. May all that we do shine a light and glorify You, so that even the blind may see and our city may be transformed.

6 Flash forth lightning and scatter them; Shoot out Your arrows and destroy them.

> We are totally dependent on Your power to strike fear in the hearts of those who oppose Your plans for our city. This fear comes from hearing an army, fully armed and quickly approaching. As vividly as a flash of lightning, make Your presence known. Rout Your enemies in glorious defeat. Scatter those who oppose You.

7 Stretch out Your hand from above; rescue me and deliver me out of great waters, from the hand of foreigners,

> When the task of City Transformation becomes overwhelming and we find ourselves in impossible situations, reach Your hand down from heaven and rescue us, O Lord. When the flood waters of adversity are raging, when the enemy is rejoicing at our calamity, and when the hearts of the people are as far from us as if they were born

in another country, deliver us for Your Name's sake.

8 Whose mouth speaks lying words, and whose right hand is a right hand of falsehood.

During this City Transformation process, there will be people in the city who will protect their interests by spreading rumors and falsehoods while extending the right hand of fellowship. We cannot become suspicious of the motives of people without jeopardizing our mission. God, give us wisdom to see the truth. Expose their deceitfulness.

9 I will sing a new song to You, O God; on a harp of ten strings I will sing praises to You,

We praise You, O Lord, always. When we see Your face, when we feel Your presence, when we trust in Your word, we praise You. We praise You for allowing us to be a significant part of Your kingdom plans. Through our successes, we will lead others to praise the name above all names — the name of Jesus.

10 The One who gives salvation to kings, who delivers David His servant from the deadly sword.

There is no power on earth that can stop Your plans. Victory is certain when the Lord gives it. We cannot fail. We trust You to deliver us from those who threaten our lives. Lord, do not allow the enemy to claim victory by taking our lives in the battle for the soul of our city.

11 Rescue me and deliver me from the hand of foreigners, whose mouth speaks lying words, and whose right hand is a right hand of falsehood —

As we implement City Transformation strategies, this is our second warning to watch for those who claim to be our friends, but whose heart is far from You. They oppose You by speaking lies. We want to trust what people say, so please, protect us from false friends and deceitful people. Lord, do not trust that we are discerning enough to always know who they are. Rescue us from them.

12 That our sons may be as plants grown up in their youth; that our daughters may be as pillars, sculptured in palace style;

> Lord, help us keep our eye on the prize. Our children are the most significant legacy of our time on earth. As parents, we want to see them grow and prosper. When a plant is full grown, it is lush and fruitful. May our sons grow up to do exactly what You created them to be and do.

> When the corner pillars are cut, they are cut perfectly to provide the point of reference from which the rest of the structure is measured. May our daughters be cornerstones of our city where absolute truth can be found.

> By our faithfulness to follow Your plans for our city, may our children have all the right nutrients, all the right building materials, to grow strong, healthy, and righteous. Help them to thrive and glorify You with the fruit of their lives.

13 That our barns may be full, supplying all kinds of produce; that our sheep may bring forth thousands and ten thousands in our fields;

> A city that follows Your plans will prosper. There is abundance of every kind. It is in our best interest as a city to individually and collectively follow Your plans and purposes. The result is that our citizens will prosper. Jobs will be plentiful, businesses will thrive, food and other resources will abound. May it be so in Tucson, Arizona, O Lord.

14 That our oxen may be well laden; that there be no breaking in or going out; that there be no outcry in our streets.

When our ways please You Lord, You protect our families and businesses as we follow Your plans. You will protect against misfortune, failure and shortage. It is a blessing from You when the needs of people are met by Your abundance and when they are able to live comfortably in their homes. Lord, make Your plans succeed through us as we are faithful to You. Misfortune will not befall us; blessings will abound. People in the community will have their needs met and not resort to protesting and rioting in the streets. Lord, may our blessings be evident to all.

15 Happy are the people who are in such a state; happy are the people whose God is the LORD!

Lord, when Your blessings fall on us, our citizens will be happy and fulfilled. Happiness of this kind only comes as people recognize their need for You, Lord, and decide to follow Your ways. Following Your ways is the secret to true happiness. The righteous in a city determine the level of blessings the city receives. Thus, the people are happy and blessed when Your people are in authority.

As we pray for city transformation, it is wise to align our strategies and tactics as closely as possible with what we know God wants. It is the only way we can be confident that we are working with God, not against Him. Psalm 144 serves as an encouragement to me as we persevere in our work through 4Tucson.

It is up to us as citizens of the kingdom of God to live out His plans in such a way as to bring blessings upon this city. It is His plan, and our willingness to live them out, that will transform our city. The result will be joy, abundance, and the cup of our city overflowing. While it will always be an imperfect world, our city will one day shine like a light in the darkness, honoring our Lord until that final day. Many people will choose to follow Jesus because they will have evidence that His ways work best.

Questions to ponder:

- What does City Transformation look like to you?
- If you could change anything you wanted to change in your city and money was no object, what would you attempt for God?
- How would you know when you got there?
- What measures will you use to gauge your impact?
- What are you diligently praying for God to do in your city?

CHAPTER 7
The 4Tucson Model

Eye has not seen, nor ear heard, nor have entered into the heart of man
the things which God has prepared for those who love Him.
1 Corinthians 2:9

When any group of city leaders attempt to create an operational model for city transformation, they should spend an extended period of time in prayer, asking God for clarity about what He wants to accomplish in their city. This process of hearing from God could easily take more than a year of regularly meeting together, researching your city's problems, and praying for strategy to solve them. In our "hurry up and get something done" culture, being patient will be the hardest part of creating a model for your city. As you study and research the most difficult problems of your city, God will reveal a list of ideas He wants to do in your city. From that list, city leaders will need to develop the **Why**, the **Vision**, the **Mission**, and the **Strategy** for accomplishing the things He has called Christians in your city to do. It would be wise not to move forward until those four areas are clearly defined. If you are tempted to shortcut the process to get something started, you will pay for it later. As your city movement grows and more people get involved, it will become painfully obvious where you did not spend enough time developing your model. The less clearly the Why, Vision, Mission, and Strategy are developed; the more conflict will arise on your team. The lack of clarity will inevitably show up in disunity. To keep conflict at a minimum it is best to think through, as much as possible, what God is calling you to do and how you intend to accomplish the task. Try to identify potential areas of conflict before enlisting more leaders, staff, or volunteers into your organizational model.

Another problem that may surface, different from charging ahead with only a half-baked plan, is that city transformation is multifaceted. Conflict may also arise from the reality that most churches and nonprofits only have experience working with one primary focus. Nonprofits form to create reading programs, help tutor students, feed the homeless, work with single mothers or orphans, drill water wells, or provide emergency relief for those in need. There will be many other singularly focused problems in your city that deserve attention. City Transformation includes all those things and a hundred more. City Transformation is, by necessity, complicated and multidimensional. Our definition of **City Transformation is bringing all the structures and institutions of the city into alignment with biblical principles for the peace and prosperity of its citizens.**

For many Christians who are accustomed to a singularly focused ministry, City Transformation will be overwhelming. Be warned, there will be a lot of well-intentioned Christians who will want to reshape the Vision and Mission into something more manageable and simpler to understand — usually wanting to focus on one singular problem at a time. Most Christians have not been trained to think strategically about the whole city. The 4Tucson model is the result of taking something extremely complex and making it easier to be understood by larger groups of Christians. As mentioned earlier, if our model can help leaders in your city — use it. If we can help you think through some particularly difficult areas of your city, feel free to contact us. Our contact information is located in the back of the book. We will do our best to help you. We are all working for the same King and want to advance His kingdom.

The Why
While we did not recognize this at first, we later realized we were continually

in discussions with Christian leaders, talking about "why" Christians should be involved in City Transformation at all. Secondarily, we found ourselves trying to help Jesus followers understand that we had the best hope to successfully fulfill the mandates of God if we would work together. We believe the 4Tucson model offers a biblical strategy for city transformation that allows each partner to determine the role he/she wants to play.

If we were starting over again, we would focus more on the "why" at the very beginning rather than the "what" (vision and mission) or "how" (strategy). After frequently exploring key scriptures with ministry leaders, our "why" developed into a clear, compelling, biblical rationale for 4Tucson.

The "Why" of 4Tucson
- We believe God created the world and everything in it to bring glory to Himself. (John 1:1-14 & Colossians 1:16)
- We believe God gave mankind the Bible to give us wisdom and teach godly principles that, when followed, maximize God's blessings to people and brings glory to Him. (Ephesians 3:10, Psalm 64:9)
- We believe Christians collectively, as a body, bring glory to God by serving together in unity, applying biblical principles to make a positive difference in our community. (John 17 & Psalm 145:6)
- We believe Christians individually receive the greatest blessings from God and cause others to glorify Him when they serve others in His name. (Matthew 5:16 & I Timothy 6:18)

THEREFORE, every Christian should be involved in 4Tucson.

The Vision
A vision statement of the organization should answer the question, "what?" It is your preferred future or ideal end result. It should be the north star

that leads your organization, reflecting your values and beliefs and that compellingly inspires and challenges.

The *Vision* of 4Tucson
To serve as a catalyst to engage the Christian community in bringing about spiritual and societal transformation for the prosperity of the entire community.

The Mission
A mission statement should answer the question, "how?" It should be a flexible framework that helps your organization stay focused on what it does, who it does it for, and how it does what it does.

The *Mission* of 4Tucson
To partner with every sector and domain of society based on common love, common goals, and the common good to make Tucson one of the most livable cities in the world, allowing each partner to determine the part it should play.

The Strategy
A strategy is your defined plan of action for achieving your Vision and Mission. We have found it helpful to state our strategy in the form of a Unique Selling Proposition or USP. In the marketing world, a USP is a pithy way to communicate how your strategy is unique (i.e.: we are the only ones doing this). It serves to differentiate in a clear and understandable way the mission of one organization from any other organization in the city. Because one of the keys to City Transformation is unity of the body of Christ, trying to articulate the strategy of 4Tucson without alienating all the other Christian ministries in the city was a considerable challenge. We wanted to honor those ministries for making a positive difference in the lives of people in most need of their services. We regularly pray for the success of those ministries. However, without being offensive to other ministries, we needed to communicate to the

Christian community and to the city at large why 4Tucson was different from other ministries in the city. If we could not articulate why we were unique, we would not be able to recruit Christians to our cause. Because all parts of the body of Christ are needed and critical for city transformation, we wanted to take every precaution not to appear to demean the work of other ministries in developing our USP. The USP is our statement of differentiation.

> **The *Strategy* of 4Tucson — USP: (Unique Selling Proposition)**
> 4Tucson's strategy is to address our city's most difficult and systemic problems by uniting Christians to envision and implement biblical solutions for the benefit of the whole city.

Our Two Part Strategy - Domains and Taskforces
In order for the 4Tucson strategy to work effectively it was necessary to have two distinct parts. Both serve a unique function and both are critical to the success of City Transformation. The two parts of the strategy are the Domains and the Taskforces.

Part 1: The Domain Strategy
No one person is smart enough to have all the answers to every problem facing our city. However, by collaboratively working together, each individual brings a piece of the solution to the table. Everyone sees the problem from their own unique expertise or experience.

You may remember the movie Apollo 13. The space capsule needed a CO_2 filter to prevent the asphyxiation of the astronauts. At the Johnson Space Center, a box of parts that were available on the space craft were dumped on a table. A group of scientists and engineers were given the task of making a filter from the parts that would work before the astronauts ran out of air. Together they accomplished what would have been impossible for any individual person to design on their own, no matter how smart. But by collaborating, they found a solution just in time.

The collective IQ of a group trying to solve a problem will always be greater than the IQ of any single individual within that group. We have learned we need the wisdom and perspective of each other. The Domains are designed to tap into that collective genius within our Christian community. By allowing believers to associate with other Christians around the city, building relationships, sharing common experiences, passions and unique knowledge, the people in each Domain will gain a unique perspective of a problem and offer key parts of the solution.

We identified *12 Domains*, or spheres of influence, within our city where Christians are already actively involved. Through the Domains, we train Christians to use their spiritual gifts, talents, and passions to make a positive difference in their circles of influence for the glory of God.

The 12 Domains of 4Tucson are designed to network the Kingdom of God across denominational and racial/cultural lines through regular *Fellowship* meetings. As Christians gather in one of the Domains, they meet other Christians in the city and become aware of city problems unique to their Domain. Each Domain may create or participate in *Programs* and *Projects* that take advantage of opportunities to solve problems that alleviate the

pain and suffering of a particular group of people. To leverage their impact, Domains create Strategic Alliances with church ministries and other nonprofits who may already be working to solve a specific problem. Where there is no ministry working on a particular problem, the Domains may find it necessary to create a program or project to address a specific need within the community.

One example of creating a program because there was a need, occurred when many of the schools in our area began to lose funding. Programs like art, music, sports, and after school tutoring were cut out of school budgets. Facilities maintenance was deferred until better financial times returned. There were Christians coming together through efforts like the "Eleven-Eleven Project" to pray for schools. There were also existing programs to engage churches through "Serve our Schools" or "Make a Difference Day."

When the school budget crisis was at a critical stage, our Education and Church Domain Directors went to the leadership of the local school districts and asked, "How can we pray for you?" and "How can we help?" Their offers of help were at first met with skepticism and suspicion. However, as we were faithful to meet school needs as they were presented, the Christian community was given more and more opportunities to serve. This is an example of what Eric Swanson explained in his book. Service is the sweet spot. We served the schools to the best of our ability without a hidden agenda. 4Tucson was catalytic in offering trainings to churches who wanted to partner with a neighborhood school. The more we served, the more we found the school districts wanting to expand the number of school/church partnerships. Three years later, more than 80% of our public schools, more than 150 schools, have a school/church partnership. Thousands of volunteer hours and thousands of dollars have flowed from local churches into neighborhood public schools. In many schools, academic achievement increased and the suffering of students and families was reduced, simply because the Christian community was willing to serve others in Jesus' name.

Part 2: The Taskforce Strategy

The second part of the 4Tucson Strategy is the *Taskforces*. By reviewing 30 years of strategies and strategic plans of our city, we were able to identify chronic, systemic, multi-generational problems that our city, up to this point, had not been able to fix. From those documents we identified and itemized 22 of the most difficult and systemic problems facing our city. We then compared that list of problems with the mandates of God. To the surprise of many Christians, there was a strong correlation between what the city leaders wanted for our citizens and what God wanted for people living in His kingdom.

We took the 22 city-wide problems and grouped them into three broad categories; **Moral and Cultural Heritage**; **Community and Family Stability**; and **City Infrastructure**. We call these 22 city problems Strategic Focus Areas. Each Taskforce is then responsible for researching, developing, and implementing biblical solutions for each of the focus areas. As a side note, these are specific problems facing Tucson. After praying and researching your city, you will most likely come up with a completely different list.

4Tucson's Strategic Focus Areas are

Moral and Cultural Heritage	Community and Family Stability	City Infrastructure
1. World View	1. Marriage	1. Water
2. Meta-Narrative	2. Parenting	2. Energy
3. City Awareness of Positive Christian Value	3. Education	3. Transportation
4. Normative to go to Church	4. Health & Healthcare	4. Access to Capital
5. Racial Reconciliation	5. Poverty Reduction	5. Economic Opportunity & Development
6. Pro-Family Government	6. Housing	6. Natural Resource Management
	7. Family Legacy	7. Land Use
	8. Quality of Life	
	9. Fun Place to Live	

4Tucson Taskforces are made up of Christian volunteers from each of the Domains who are committed to building working partnerships with local churches, nonprofits and agencies that are equally committed to solving specific city problems. We often say to other organizations and agencies, "You don't have to believe like we believe to care about what we care about." Our plan is to solve city problems with biblical solutions and we will work with anyone who is willing to pull on the same end of the rope.

There are two points we need to clarify here. The first point is when a problem is identified, it must be researched and a biblical Action Plan developed. The research should identify the structural and institutional misalignments with God's word. The Action Plan should explain how to address the barriers that would prohibit a biblical solution to the problem from being implemented. Creating the Action Plan is where the collective IQ of Domains begins to show its true potential. People with knowledge and expertise in each Domain will see the problem from different perspectives. For example: If the problem to be solved is homelessness (which is not one of our 22), each Domain would look at the solution differently. The Business Domain might say the solution is for the homeless to get a job. The Education Domain might say to solve the problem, the homeless need more education. The Social Services Domain might say the homeless need a hand-up, not a hand-out. The Healthcare Domain might have the perspective that the homeless have mental illnesses that needs to be addressed. The Government Domain might see the solution involving programs that would move the homeless from the streets to apartments or to houses. The Church Domain might believe the problem is the homeless need Jesus.

None of these perspectives are wrong, they are just incomplete. By collaborating together with Christians from each Domain, every perspective is valued and considered. As the biblical Action Plan is created, it will be more balanced, sustainable, and have fewer unintended consequences.

The second point of clarification is there are already people and organizations working to solve the problem you are interested in solving. If your city is like Tucson, you will discover there is very little coordination between organizations serving the same populations or attempting to solve similar problems. More often than not, one organization is not aware another organization with a similar passion even exists. In Tucson, we have more than 3,400 nonprofits. That is one nonprofit for every 300 people in our city. These organizations are focused and working hard to solve a very specific problem they recognize within the community. These organizations and ministries are also competing with each other for funding and volunteers. Fishing from the same small pond potentially creates other conflicts between organizations.

In researching a city problem, it is critical to identify all of the organizations, agencies, and key people working on the problem you have identified. You will need to know which specific part of the problem they are working on, how they are funded, how many people are involved with them, etc. One of the advantages of asking everyone to consider working with 4Tucson is that we have become the neutral convener that is helping develop a comprehensive city-wide plan. As we successfully implement the plan, we are able to help many other Christian nonprofit organizations in the city with funding and volunteers. We are not interested in reinventing the wheel. Where there is an area in the Action Plan not being addressed, the role of 4Tucson is then to develop a program or project with trained and engaged Christians who are motivated to fill that void. Collectively, the Christian community begins to systemically solve one city problem after another with biblical solutions.

Here are the steps we took to develop biblical solutions for city problems.
1. **Review and Understand 4Tucson's Vision Statement.**
   - We see 4Tucson serving as a catalyst to engage the Christian community to bring about spiritual and societal transformation for the benefit of the entire city.
2. **Review and Understand 4Tucson's Mission Statement.**

- We will partner with every sector and domain of society based on common love, common goals, and the common good to make Tucson one of the most livable cities in the world, allowing each partner to determine the part he or she should play.

3. **Review 4Tucson's Strategic Plan and the 22 Key City-Wide Areas of Focus.**
    - Review the Definition and Challenge/Issue of the specific Taskforce.
    - Understand the Goal (outcome) of the Taskforce.

4. **Research the issue and the differing views of the Key Area of Focus of the Taskforce.**
    - Research books, internet, newspapers, magazines, city reports. Document all research.
    - Save all articles and research reports and organize them by categories.

5. **Research who are the key players in the Key Area of Focus in our city. Identify key people in the city who are directly working on or with this issue.**
    - Identify second tier people who are working behind the scenes on the issue.

6. **Research what are the key agencies that receive grant money or fund the work on the Key Area of Focus.**
    - Identify all nonprofit organizations who receive money to work on the issue.

        How much do they receive?

        Where does the money come from?

        How many people are on their staff?

        Who is the Executive Director?

        Who serves on the Board of the organization?

    - Identify key businesses that either work on the issue or provide financial resources for it.

7. **Research the plans, blueprints, and strategies of the city around the Key Area of Focus.**

    - Identify who are the key city leaders who are passionate about the problem.
    - Which city leaders are neutral about the problem?
    - Which city leaders or staff personnel will be an obstacle to any solution for solving the problem?

8. **Research what the Bible says about the Key Area of Focus and the problem being solved. (The reason we put this as step 8 is because the research in the previous steps will help you better define the problem and will guide you to the key principles and precepts in the Bible)**

    - Does God care about this problem and why?
    - Identify biblical principles that apply to the issue or problem.
    - Identify key Bible passages that address the issue directly.
    - What is the theological rational for getting involved in solving the issue or problem?

9. **Research Christian organizations and/or individuals who are passionate about the Key Area of Focus.**

    - Identify Christian nonprofit organizations who raise money to work on the issue.

      How much do they receive?

      Where does the money come from?

      How many people are on their staff?

      Who is the Executive Director?

      Who serves on the Board of the organization?

    - Identify Christian nonprofits collaborating to solve the problem.

10. **Research the scope and measure of the Key Area of Focus.**

    - How many people does this problem impact?
    - How is the size or impact of the problem currently measured?

- Who measures it and how often?
- Are those measuring the issue measuring the right things?
- How are the measurements reported?
- How widely are they reported?
- Who pays to measure? Who pays for the report?
- How is success determined?

11. **Research the structures and institutions that may negatively impact the Key Area of Focus.**
    - What specific laws or city policies negatively impact the desired change?
    - Who are the key leaders who may initiate changes in the laws of our city?

Questions to prayerfully consider in bringing Christians together for City Transformation:
- What is the meaning of John 17?

    Who is Jesus praying for?

    Who is Jesus not praying for?

    Why is He praying for us?

    How does John 17 apply to Christian involvement in our city?

    Read the book, Jesus' Surprising Strategy by David Drum

    Read Dave's sequel book, If It Were Easy, Jesus Wouldn't Have Prayed for It.

- What is the meaning of Matthew 5:13-16?

    How does this passage apply to Christian involvement in our city?

- What is the meaning of Matthew 28:19-20?

    How does this passage apply to Christian involvement in our city?

CHAPTER 8
The 4Tucson Schematic

To what shall we liken the kingdom of God?
Or with what parable shall we picture it?
Mark 4:30

The following images are designed to help anyone who may be considering using the 4Tucson model in their city. A picture may help you visually understand what you have read about 4Tucson so far. The version we share in our presentations is animated, so you will need to use your imagination.

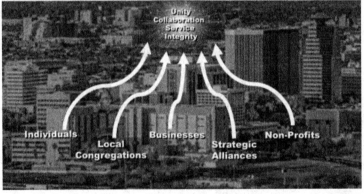

A biblical city transformational movement begins with God calling Christians across the city individually, gathering local congregations, calling kingdom businesses and calling Christian nonprofits and developing intentional strategic alliances with other agencies in the city.

When those Christians agree to work together for the benefit of the city through unity, collaboration, service and integrity, their collective light starts to shine for others to see.

Focused Light Becomes Powerful

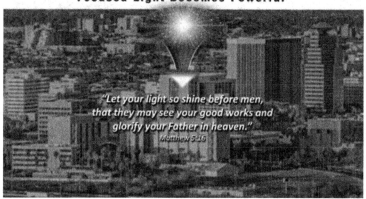

"Let your light so shine before men, that they may see your good works and glorify your Father in heaven."
Matthew 5:16

A laser is focused light and is extremely powerful. God calls us to let our light so shine before men, that they may see your good works and glorify your Father in heaven (Matthew 5:16). The problem in our generation is Christians have largely let their light shine wherever they are able within their circles of influence, but they have seldom combined their light with the light of other believers. Their light individually, while important to shine, is more like a candle. One single candle can offer hope in a dark world and people are drawn to its light. However, in John 17 we find Jesus praying for the unity of His followers to serve as evidence that He was sent by the Father (John 17:21). By working together, our light becomes significantly more powerful. Through the power of our lights shining together with laser-like precision, we are able to see visible transformation take place. When that happens, people begin to praise our Heavenly Father for the work we do together.

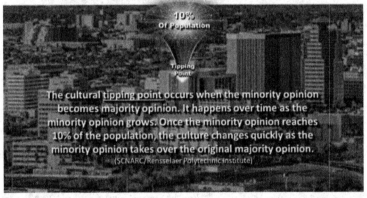

Enough Light Causes a Cultural Tipping Point

10%
Of Population

Tipping
Point

The cultural tipping point occurs when the minority opinion becomes majority opinion. It happens over time as the minority opinion grows. Once the minority opinion reaches 10% of the population, the culture changes quickly as the minority opinion takes over the original majority opinion.
(SCNARC/Rensselaer Polytechnic Institute)

A research report by Rensselaer Polytechnic Institute found that when 10% of the population of any group shares and strongly believes a particular viewpoint, their view quickly becomes the majority view.

As Christians, we believe the ways of God work best in every area of life. As of this writing, that is not the majority view of the population of our city. Our goal is to reach that 10% tipping point where our minority view of God's ways is adopted and becomes the majority view of our city. It is called the Cultural Tipping Point.

The population of Tucson is just under one million people. Ten percent of one million is 100,000 people. Our goal is to get 10% of the population of Tucson to agree to work together to apply biblical principles to the most difficult and systemic problems of our city. It is interesting to note that 78% of the people in Tucson, about 780,000 people, claim to be Christians. We believe God's ways are most powerfully seen when we work together collectively. Then, through us, God is able to display His power and bless the people in our city.

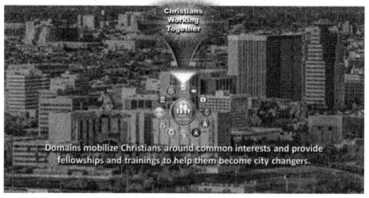

Light Gathers in the 12 DOMAINS

Christians Working Together

Domains mobilize Christians around common interests and provide fellowships and trainings to help them become city changers.

We have observed that the majority of Christians in Tucson don't know each other. We have taken the three sectors of society, the public sector, the private sector and the social sector, and divided them into 12 smaller circles of influence called Domains.

Our 12 Domains are: Business, Education, Church, Government, Prayer, Social Services, Healthcare, Justice, Media & Arts, Sports, Environment, and Philanthropy. The Domains provide opportunities for Christians to gather around a common interest. They meet each other in fellowship gatherings. As they begin to study city problems, they take personal responsibility for them. Members of the Domains want to use their spiritual gifts, their talents, and their financial resources to solve city problems. The Domains are where Christians get to know each other and look for opportunities to use gifts and abilities to make positive differences in the city.

Taskforces Address 22 City Problems

In Tucson, Arizona, we studied more than 30 years' worth of city blueprints, strategic plans and various city initiatives which attempted to solve the problems of the city. Most failed and others created unintended consequences, thereby hurting one group of people by trying to help another group.

Out of those city blueprints, strategic plans and initiatives, we were able to identify systemic problems that were perpetuated generation after generation. We also researched the Bible to identify the mandates of God that directly impacted those difficult problems. From that exercise, we were able to identify 22 key city-wide problems that must be fixed if our city is to thrive and prosper as God intended.

We call these 22 problems Strategic Focus Areas. From the Domains, we recruit and train Christians who have a passion and interest in fixing one of the 22 problems. We then conduct a research report that outlines the problem and its causes with verifiable data.

Once the research report is complete, a Taskforce is created. The Taskforce is charged with taking the data and creating an Action Plan to solve the problem with a biblical solution.

Often the Action Plan will have several key elements that concentrate on smaller pieces of the problem to be solved. Transformation Teams, smaller groups within the Taskforce, are created where Christians are further trained to focus on solving one small piece of the bigger problem. When taken collectively with the other Transformation Teams, the goals and objectives outlined in the Action Plan are reached. The city problem is solved with a biblical solution. Structures and Institutions are changed to sustain the implemented solution. By letting our light shine together, letting our city see our good works (biblical solutions), the citizens praise our Father in Heaven.

Body of Christ in Action

As the body of Christ works collectively in unity, it is taking responsibility for the most difficult and systemic problems of our city. When our love for people compels to us to use God's wisdom to create biblical solutions that will help the people in our city — it is at that point the explosive power of God is on full display through us.

2 Corinthians 4:7 says, "But we have this treasure (God's wisdom and supremacy) in earthen vessels, that the excellence of the power may be of God and not of us." (parenthesis added).

The Greek word for the power of God is dunamis. It is the root word from which we get our English word dynamite. The power of God is the most powerful force known to mankind.

Our treasure is the power and wisdom Jesus Christ gives to us, His ambassadors. Our treasure is the transformational power of God at work within our earthen vessels. Our treasure is the manifold wisdom of God being made known to our city.

When the power of God is on display through the body of Christ, explosively powerful transformation happens as a result.

As Christians implement biblical solutions through Domains and Taskforces, the power of God begins to change and then transform the structures and institutions of our city. City structures are the policies and laws governing the behavior of the citizens. The city institutions are the mores and values of the culture. Structures may be changed relatively quickly. Institutions are the gatekeepers and protectors of the culture and therefore change more slowly.

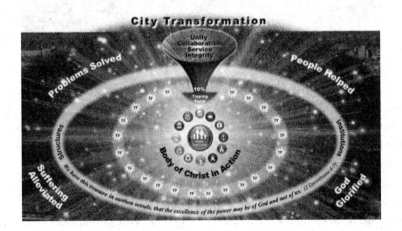

Biblical City Transformation happens when the explosive power of God impacts the structures and institutions of the city to bring them into alignment with biblical principles. When structures and institutions follow God's wisdom, the largest number of people possible will be helped and they will praise God for His goodness.

When a city follows biblical principles, the power of God is on display for all to see.

- Systemic and difficult problems are solved,
- People are helped,
- Suffering is alleviated, and
- God is glorified.

CHAPTER 9

The 3P's — The People

Your people shall be volunteers in the day of Your power;
in the beauties of holiness, from the womb of the morning,
You have the dew of Your youth.
Psalm 110:3

Marcus Lemonis, the host of the TV show, "The Profit", says he judges all businesses by the 3P's: People, Process, and Product. He says the most important "P" is people. The right people are effective, while the wrong people are destructive. The second "P" is process. Processes determine how an organization creates, delivers, and markets their products. Finally, the third "P" determines whether the product itself is excellent and relevant. I would like to use the 3P's as a template to further explain the 4Tucson Model.

I agree with Marcus that people are critically important. For our discussion of city transformation, we need to consider two groups of people: staff and volunteers. When I first started publicly sharing the 4Tucson Vision, it was just that — a vision — a concept. When 4Tucson began, every leadership position was held by a committed volunteer.

For example, our first volunteer Church Domain Director was a godly man named Dick Buus. Dick served on a local church staff and dedicated as much time as he was able to volunteering with 4Tucson. He was instrumental in gathering pastors on a monthly basis to advocate for the idea that by working together, churches could do so much more for the kingdom of God in our city.

Dick was followed by local retired pastor, Tim Coop. Tim started taking the interested pastors through a process of learning to see the city as their mission field. Tim later moved to Las Vegas to be closer to family. The Church Domain Position remained vacant for several months. Volunteers worked hard with the hours available, but city transformation is full-time work.

It was not until 4Tucson's first full-time Domain Director came on board that we began actually developing the model to a point where we could share it with the Christian community. David Drum had been a Lutheran pastor at the same church for 25 years. He and I had discussed the vision of 4Tucson from time to time at some of the pastor gatherings. One day Dave came to me and said, *"I believe God is calling me to serve at 4Tucson as the Church Domain Director."* We laugh about it now, but at the time I said, *"That is great Dave, but I have no money to pay you. Being a Domain Director is a full-time job, with long hours, no processes in place and no support. Still want the job?"*

Dave had some loyal and faithful friends who were Kingdom servants who agreed to pay his salary for the first year. It took tremendous courage and faith for Dave to trust the provision of God by taking a full-time job with 4Tucson. It took an equal amount of faith for those supporting him financially to trust a vision that had no people, processes, or product. I will be forever grateful for those who demonstrated their faith in God and were willing to invest in something they could not yet see.

Karen Graham, a prayer intercessor in our city, agreed to volunteer as our first Prayer Domain Director. After serving several months, she said, "Mark, I am not the right person to be the Prayer Domain Director. I am resigning that position for whomever God is preparing to take that role."

It wasn't long after Dave became our first full-time Director that Brian Goodall came on board full-time as the Prayer Domain Director. Very soon after Brian joined our team, Bernadette Gruber became our first full-time

Education Domain Director. Brian and Bernadette also had to raise their own salary support. Dave, Brian and Bernadette all had families with children at various ages from elementary school to college. Joining 4Tucson was no small commitment on their part. It is one thing for someone to say they have faith that God will provide, but very few Christians actually have the courage to put their family's welfare on the line to see if it is true. All three were willing to take the risk, trusting God to provide for their families and as a result, each witnessed firsthand the faithfulness of God in action.

All four of us agreed that the vision was compelling and the cause was biblical. However, there were times when it was very difficult to keep moving forward when everyone on staff was frantically trying to raise money to feed their families, pay for health insurance, and keep their cars running in between meetings with city leaders. Not one of our 4Tucson staff complained. They continued to do their best. They set appointments with key leaders in the city to influence their decisions in a godly direction. God proved Himself faithful over and over to each of them, providing for their needs monthly. Because of their daring, 4Tucson was on its way moving from a vision into a developing city transformational strategy. I am personally grateful for the testimony of faith of Dave, Brian, and Bernadette. They have been great examples to me and have proven time after time that they are faithful warriors on the frontlines of our city's culture wars.

The first couple of years developing and implanting the 4Tucson model were tough. Creating something from nothing takes very special people. Karen Graham, our former Prayer Domain Director, recruited John and Susan Mitchell to join her to pray regularly for 4Tucson in general and for me specifically. She asked me to join the three of them monthly for prayer, to appeal to God for wisdom and provision as we moved forward. To encourage intercessors in other cities, I asked Karen to share how God impressed her to intercede for 4Tucson. She said, "God had given me a call and heart for the city. When I saw the richness and humility of Pastor Mark, combined with his vision for Tucson, it was clear that God was positioning me to serve in intercession. Mark graciously agreed to meet with us monthly so we could stay current with prayer needs, as well as to hear how the Lord was answering our prayers throughout the month."

John was involved in the earliest discussions about forming a Board of Directors. I had hoped he would serve as one of our first board members. Instead, he explained to the exploratory group, "Through my brief board level involvement, I have come to understand a much greater vision and commitment that Mark has for the Tucson area. It is through this experience that I have come to believe that the success of 4Tucson is going to come through intercession — not just for the organization, but for Mark personally. That's where I am needed most."

Karen, John, and Susan prayed together with me monthly. We prayed through the obstacles that we continually encountered that arose from the process of starting something new. I asked Susan to share why she was so committed to pray for me. She said, "I was inspired many years ago to pray for cities after reading the book, That None Should Perish by Ed Silvoso. The vision and plan the Lord gave Pastor Mark for Tucson, along with his integrity and heart for the city, was amazing. I knew the Lord was giving me an assignment to specifically cover him in prayer and intercession as he began to move toward the vision the Lord had purposed for him to accomplish."

I can say without hesitation that it has been their faithfulness to pray with me regularly and my seeing God continually answering our prayers, that has sustained me through the most stressful times of starting 4Tucson. My intercessors were also able to witness firsthand the results of our prayers as God answered one petition after another, month after month.

Within the first year of God bringing the first three Domain Directors, He also brought Paul Parisi to be Government Domain Director. Paul got involved politically as a union shop steward and later in life was elected to the Oro Valley City Council. He really understands how the government functions. Francine Rienstra became the Media & Arts Domain Director. She had started a successful radio station in Tucson and was very familiar with how the media industry worked. Linda Goode was next to join the team as the Philanthropy Domain Director. She was passionate about helping people learn biblical generosity and had a passion to build a culture of generosity in our city. The Domains began to take shape gathering Christians within each of the spheres of influence.

The next group of special people God assembled was our first Board of Directors. Not only where these men and women volunteers, they had to make a significant financial contribution annually to serve as a board member. In order for 4Tucson to become a legitimate influencer in the city, we needed the wisdom of a group of men and women who were unafraid to invest their time, talent and treasure into something that had never seen tried before. The first Board of Directors, under the chairmanship of Doug Martin, was made up of local business and community leaders who helped 4Tucson formally organize into an approved 501(c)3 nonprofit. In the beginning, the men and women who made up the board didn't have much evidence the 4Tucson model would work. However, they were willing to risk their reputations and their financial resources to provide support for a fragile organization with a big dream. I am so grateful for godly Board members who came along side me, prayed for 4Tucson, and helped us stay afloat financially.

As God was adding key city leaders to our board and bringing key staff to our team, I focused on sharing the 4Tucson message with local pastors in our city. I found many of them had the same attitude that I had had the first ten years of my ministry. They did not play well with others. Inviting them to come together in unity around a common City Transformation Strategy was not an easy pitch. It was even harder to persuade pastors to allow members of their congregations to volunteer with 4Tucson. Early on I was hopeful pastors would be the early adopters of the 4Tucson strategy; with only a few exceptions, that did not happen.

Christian business leaders were actually the early adopters who first joined as volunteers in the movement. Business people are wired to envision and create solutions. They are not intimidated by a bold vision and they could see the power of Christians coming together to solve city problems. They believed the Bible had answers for those problems, but they had also seen many attempts by other well-meaning Christians through the years that had failed. Nevertheless, many were willing to take a chance that the 4Tucson model might work.

From the business community, leaders began to emerge. One leader who came on staff from the business community was Rick Stertz. Rick owned a contracting company and became the first full-time Executive Director. He helped introduce the vision to a wider city audience. Terri Proud then took the Executive Director's chair and helped develop our city-wide messaging. Soon after Terri's tenure, I was asked by the board to become the full-time Executive Director, a role in which I still serve today.

We continued inviting more Christians to get involved. Relying on previous personal experience gleaned from working within the city, Christian leaders offered justifiable reasons why they would not join 4Tucson. Christian educators and school administrators were originally fearful of partnering with us for fear of crossing some imaginary line between church and state. Government leaders, the gatekeepers of many of the structures and institutions, were not receptive to biblical concepts that might not be popular with their constituents. Faithful prayer warriors had prayed for years for God to transform our city, but some of them began pushing against the 4Tucson model asking why there was a need for a specific Prayer Domain. After all they reasoned, *"Shouldn't prayer be in everything?"* Even with a few full-time staff serving as city missionaries, getting Christians across the city to work together through 4Tucson proved hard work.

As we continued to build the foundation for our strategy, God began to bring additional Christian leaders from different walks of life who were willing to fill open Domain Director positions. As the 4Tucson model progressed, Domains that had influential and gifted leaders often moved into other positions of leadership as needed within the organization. For example, Tony Simms came on the team as our third Business Domain Director. Tony is one of those unique individuals who can take a vision and develop the processes that will allow it to grow. Because of his skillset, we promoted Tony from Business Domain Director to the COO position because developing processes became the most critical need at that stage of our development. We continually move our key leaders into different roles to keep us moving forward.

From the start, 4Tucson was highly entrepreneurial in how we gathered people and grew our influence in the city. Within the first two years, it became obvious that we had a lot of interrelated parts without much internal connectivity. Every Domain Director was building their individual Domains differently. One of the first things Tony helped us do was put together an organizational chart that was consistent with the vision and mission. In it, he identified all the key positions that were dependent on leaders who could perform the necessary tasks required for the 4Tucson model to work. He helped define the primary roles for Domain Directors, Taskforce Directors, and executive level staff. Many of the boxes on the 4Tucson organizational chart he created had no names in them. But at least we could visually see what the structure might look like when fully operational and the types of people we needed God to bring to help us get there.

The more we made progress in implementing the vision, the more we became dependent on God to provide just the right person at just the right time. When we would encounter an immovable obstacle that prevented us from growing to the next step, God would bless us with another incredibly gifted person with a heart for Him and the specific skills we needed. Two of those people were Micah Lunsford and Jennifer Dellerman. They joined our team to develop our database and operational systems, without which, we could not communicate, train, or engage our partners in the city transformation process.

Our next struggle came when we started seeing the individual partners join 4Tucson, only to get frustrated because, as an organization, we could not immediately plug them into a place of service that fit their gifts and passions. We were attracting good people to our city movement, but people joined 4Tucson ready to change the city. Because we had no process to help them find a place to serve, they were leaving out the back door as fast as we could bring them in the front door.

Again, God was good to us. He brought us another uniquely gifted person just when we needed her the most. Darcy McNaughton, like Tony, had a mind for processes. As VP of Fund and Partner Development, Darcy was given the task of plugging the back door. She went to work to create a system that was both functional in helping people find a place to serve, and scalable to serve more than 100,000 people at some point in the future.

The system also required that she create a process to help our partners receive the specific training they needed. It would be available to provide the best opportunity for them to succeed in the place of service that matched their passion and gifts. To accomplish her initial task, she started building a dedicated team of both staff and volunteers who could help her implement the processes she was creating. Without a good process and a good team, it would be next to impossible to successfully recruit new partners and help them find a place to serve as city changers.

A second task assigned to Darcy was to build a process for Fund Development. With the high caliber of people God continued to bring into 4Tucson, our confidence grew that His hand was guiding us. We are now praying for God to bring the exact right person we need to help us in the area of fund development. Mission Increase Foundation has been a great help in providing training in the area of donor development and they have helped us understand the type of person we needed for this position. Fund Development is critical for our long-term stability. Our Domain Directors are missionaries to the city. Some of them have been able to raise their salary support; others have not. The purpose of Fund Development is to allow God to raise up investors who see what He is doing through 4Tucson and who want to get in on it.

The "secret sauce" of the 4Tucson model is people. We are very intentionally developing teams of highly trained, highly committed Christian men and women who want to be used by God to make a difference in the world. At the beginning of your city effort, it could be interpreted that recruiting, mobilizing, and engaging Christians into city transformation seems to happen organically. At first it was the observation of some people on our leadership team that God spontaneously raised up key people to get done what He wanted done. That observation was only partially true. God does in fact raise up key people at key times for key purposes as we have experienced. But, I would encourage anyone involved in a city transformation movement not to confuse God organically raising up people with sustainability. The processes of keeping people moving toward a singular goal does not usually happen spontaneously. People and processes are different. Read the book of Acts for a biblical example. Paul and Barnabus are the people God raised up. The book of Acts explains the process God used to sustain His movement on earth.

Another example where God raised up key people in 4Tucson was a time when we struggled with sharing all the good things God was doing through Christians across our city with a broader audience. We wanted to spread the message to invite more Christians to get in on the fun stuff God was doing. We also felt a responsibility to tell the story of what God was doing in the city, so that others may praise Him. For that purpose, we asked Francine

Rienstra to move from the Media & Arts Domain Director to become our first Marketing Director. She put our first marketing team together and started exploring strategies for telling God's story in Tucson.

Having the right people come at just the right time has allowed us to move the vision from disorganization to a sustainable, city-changing Christian network. The people God has brought so far have been remarkable. We have been blessed to serve, not just with volunteers, but with partners. They are truly co-laborers who work side by side with us to envision and implement biblical solutions for city problems.

People matter to God and they matter to us. We believe that God has gifted people in our city to possess all the ideas, all the resources, and who will bring their own unique perspectives for the 4Tucson strategy to be successful.

It is the board members, the Domain Directors, Taskforce Directors and the 4Tucson staff who work to build the organizational processes that will support our city transformation movement for the long haul. But it is our volunteer partners who engage the city through various programs and projects that actually make the 4Tucson strategy work. Many of our volunteer partners work directly with our staff and do much of the heavy lifting behind the scenes. It is our partners who are the unsung heroes of 4Tucson. Our stated goal is to enlist 10% of Tucson's population as partners into the 4Tucson model. They are the key to successful city transformation.

The longer I am in a position of leadership within 4Tucson, the more I am in awe of all the remarkable people God has in His kingdom. He has chosen to use Christians as His change agents in the world. It is His intent to use His followers in the process of crafting sustainable, biblical city transformation. Our staff is continually building our internal policies and procedures with an eye on helping the people of God be successful in what He created them to do.

The 4Tucson model for city transformation is dependent on God raising up people who have been personally transformed by His power. Space does not permit me to list all the people God has used to grow 4Tucson to this stage. To those of you who played critical roles along the way, God knows your service to Him and I personally thank you. God has brought key people at critical times of our ministry to get us to each new place. We are optimistic about the future impact Christians will have on Tucson as God continues to call His followers to love our city in His name. God has key people ready to go in your city, too.

"Many nations shall be joined to the LORD in that day, and they shall become My people. And I will dwell in your midst. Then you will know that the LORD of hosts has sent Me to you."

Zechariah 2:11

CHAPTER 10

The 3P's — The Process

Let all things be done decently and in order.
1 Corinthians 14:40

The second "P" in the 3P's model of Marcus Lemonis is process. As God continued to add people and as we started to see success, we also found ourselves struggling with how to work together as a team. We were desperate for processes to be created and put in place, because we discovered once you grow past three people things start to get messy.

In one of our meetings, Brian Goodall coached me through one of the obstacles we were facing, "Mark, if you are going to be an effective Executive Director, you have got to help us develop into a team." He was exactly right, but remember my background. I had always done things myself. I didn't work well in the company of others. I had never developed an effective team in my life. However, I was willing to learn.

Fortunately for me, everyone else on the "team" had experience being a team player. They were just waiting for me to catch up. As Tony stepped into his role as COO, he explained, *"If we are going to have any chance of this vision being sustainable, we need to develop a strategic plan that everyone can work from."* As we worked on a plan that would allow 4Tucson to achieve its stated vision, we also worked on our processes. Learning to trust each other to be proficient within our own areas of expertise was just as important as the plan itself. We started getting better at developing into a team when all the players gained clarity of their roles and began to have confidence that everyone else on the team could fulfill their role. In that single sentence there is a lot of pain.

Developing a process was critical in helping us develop trust as a team. As our organization grew, it became increasing difficult for all the key players to be involved in every decision the organization needed to make. Internal tensions continued to rise. To alleviate the pressure, Tony pulled out the organizational chart and assigned critical boxes to those who demonstrated the aptitude and skillset to work within that box. Some boxes would remain empty until God brought the right person to work that part of the process. The more the process was defined and clarified, the easier it became to trust the other players on the team to do their part.

For the next two years, Tony and I led the Domain Directors through the process of creating a Strategic Plan to implement the 4Tucson vision. This entailed reading city documents and researching reports created by the city and county governments to identify the problems they saw and how they planned to solve them. We also looked at the various ministries of local churches and sifted through the long list of nonprofits to understand what problems they were specifically trying to solve.

As part of the Strategic Plan we searched the Scriptures to see what strategies people like Nehemiah used on his city. You may recall at that time the city walls of Jerusalem were broken down and the gates were in disrepair. Because of the condition of the city, the people were fearful of plunderers who at various times would raid the city to steal the crops and possessions of the people. Lawlessness proliferated in the community. City walls in Nehemiah's day were intended to provided strength, power, purpose and identity for the citizens. When in place, the walls empowered the people inside to thrive and reach their God given potential. When they were broken, the people were vulnerable and fearful.

City of Jerusalem
(during Nehemiah's Time)

Photo credit kzlam36.wordpress.com

Through prayer and multiple weekly conversations, we were able to define and set goals for each of the 22 Strategic Focus Areas. The Strategic Focus Areas were the systemic problem areas where, figuratively, the walls of our city were broken and our city gates were in desperate need of repair. Our city could not thrive until these breaches were repaired.

We defined each of the 22 city problems that needed a solution and wrote a biblical theology and policy statements for each one. From that, we then identified a clear goal for each of the 22 problems. See Appendix B. From the beginning, we agreed that, in order for a solution to help the most people possible, it would need to be a biblical solution. If it were not a biblical solution, we would be guilty of creating a solution from our own opinions. We believed that God's ways work best and offered the best hope to benefit the most people. We understood that the closer our solutions were aligned with what God taught in the Bible, the closer we would be to repairing the city gates and walls in a way that would allow for peace and prosperity for every person in the Tucson.

As we continued to develop the Strategic Plan for the city, it became clear to everyone on our 4Tucson team that our internal processes were also broken or nonexistent. There were many robust discussions regarding the relationship between Domains and Taskforces. We needed clarity on who had authority to make key decisions for the organization, what processes we would use for gathering data to make key decisions, and what process we would use for allowing input and incorporating diverse views to ensure the most productive outcomes. It wasn't always pleasant.

The lack of an effective process began to take its toll. We could not build our internal processes fast enough to keep up with our growth. We experienced more and more conflict within our team, even to the point where all of us considered quitting because the stress was so high.

Several meetings had to take place just to resolve hurt feelings and rifts in interpersonal relationships. We were determined to follow the conflict resolution process outlined in Scripture for times just like this. We reasoned that if we could not learn to resolve our own issues, we would have no credibility when working with people in the community to resolve city-wide issues. The good news was we were all committed to the vision and were determined to persevere though the conflict. Brian used a marriage analogy to help us gain greater insight. He said that in his marriage, divorce wasn't an option. His point was that a family works through problems. We considered our staff a family of believers. I sarcastically retorted at a particularly high point of frustration that, "If this was his idea of family, I wanted no part of it."

As we were struggling to develop our internal processes, we began to experience another problem that added to our stress. We were not raising enough money to make payroll and pay rent. At times it appeared that 4Tucson would collapse and disintegrate into ruin before we could ever get it built. We regularly prayed for God to help us hold it together while we put the supports and processes in place to sustain the organization.

In our staff meetings, we have developed a one sentence declaration we use frequently at critical junctures: *"This might be one of those times to pray."* At one point of severe stress, we asked the entire staff to fast and pray for three days. Our intent was to come together at the end of that time to discuss if it was possible to keep moving forward. We were in desperate need for God to provide financial relief.

A few days after fasting and praying, God provided us with a gift of just enough money to make it one more month. It was a great encouragement for our staff to experience firsthand God answering prayers. It also provided the hope we needed to hold on. We continue to stay focused on building what God had shown us, believing He would also provide a much needed financial breakthrough.

At the end of 2015, Tony gave us each a three-inch binder with the organizational chart separated into smaller specific parts. Most of the pages were full of red sentences. The red sentences were bullet points of all the processes that had to be created before we could move to the next level of growth. It seemed daunting; there were so many processes that needed to be created. We understood that we would continue to experience high levels of stress until they were created and adopted.

All of 2016 was about process development. Tony continually kept our focus on the type of culture we were creating by continually asking if we were being consistent with biblical principles in our development of the processes, systems, and policies. Were we honoring God in our relationships with each other and with people in the community? Darcy was in high gear creating partnership and fundraising processes that were scalable to support our growth to several thousand volunteers. On the whiteboard behind her desk was written, *"NO Band-Aids™, Build for the long-haul."* Building sustainable systems for the long-haul was the focus of everyone on the team.

Each week the whole staff of Domain Directors met to hear updates on what was going on within each Domain and to attempt to coordinate our efforts wherever possible. We started having weekly Senior Management Meetings that included the Executive Director, the COO, and the first three Domain Directors and the VP of Fund and Partner Development to create policies and procedures that would support our daily city engagement activities. It seemed every day we encountered a new set of problems that needed to be resolved before we could take the next step.

I remember becoming very familiar with praying through Lamentations 3:20-26: *"My soul still remembers and sinks within me. This I recall to my mind; therefore, I have hope. Through the LORD's mercies we are not consumed, because His compassions fail not. They are new every morning; Great is Your faithfulness. 'The LORD is my portion,' says my soul, 'Therefore I hope in Him!' The LORD is good to those who wait for Him, to the soul who seeks Him. It is good that one should hope and wait quietly for the salvation of the LORD."*

Our Domain programs and projects kept us engaged in the community while we continued to create processes that would allow for future growth. God continued to provide just what we needed, when we needed it to get us to the next step. We were learning to trust God's faithfulness at every turn. It was a long year, but we did it!

CHAPTER 11
The 3Ps — The Product

He shall be like a tree planted by the rivers of water, that brings forth its fruit in its season, whose leaf also shall not wither; and whatever he does shall prosper.

Psalm 1:3

The third and final "P" in 3P's of Marcus Lemonis, is the product. 4Tucson's product is City Transformation. We define that as bringing all city structures and institutions into alignment with biblical principles for the benefit (peace and prosperity) of the whole city. With right people and the right processes in place, we were beginning to see positive changes in our city.

It doesn't take a genius to see what is (was) broken in a city. The genius is finding effective solutions that actually fix existing city problems that are hurting people and that don't unintentionally hurt other people by creating a completely new set of problems.

To determine the success of any organization it is important to establish the criteria for measuring the actual impact it is having on a society. Success cannot be measured by good intentions. As humans we have the ability to validate our existence with anecdotal evidence. We did not want to fall into that trap at 4Tucson. We realize the validity of our implemented solutions and their impact must be evaluated, analyzed, and measured against real quantifiable data.

We decided it best to use statistics and data that the city collects and publishes so that no one can accuse us of manipulating the outcomes in our favor. There are some city problems where published, independent, third party reports are also available to measure our effectiveness. Supplying independent, measurable data to the donors who fund the vision and mission helps validate their return on investment. Measurable data also encourages Christians interested in joining 4Tucson. They want to participate in something that is working and producing positive results.

To be able to communicate where we were making a difference, we developed a purpose statement for each Domain and Taskforce with annual goals and measurable outcomes. We budget each year according to those goals. Each Domain or Taskforce has tactics, outputs and outcomes that are shared with the whole staff in weekly reports. The purpose of reporting weekly is help the team get a sense of how their individual efforts are contributing to the overall success of the organizational goals. It also helps our staff identify which team members are struggling and need help. The data from the weekly reports is compiled and evaluated quarterly. From the quarterly data, we then produce an annual report where we measure our organizational goals with the city data and communicate publicly if we were able to make a measurable difference in fixing a particular city problem. The data from the annual report is also used as a guide for setting our goals for the next year.

We have documented verifiable evidence that our Domains are significantly impacting our city. A few of those successes are shared in Appendix A at the back of this book.

Because we are just beginning to implement out Taskforce strategy, it is harder to document successes in those areas using third party data. Keep in mind, the Taskforce Action Plans may take several years to fully implement and see tangible results. There are no quick fixes for difficult and systemic problems. The point here is that in order to move closer to the defined Taskforce goals, we recognize the importance of specific measurable objectives being built into our strategy from the beginning.

Our product is City Transformation. The first Taskforce in developing that product was the Poverty Reduction Taskforce. Here is our definition of the problem, our philosophy, and goal.

> **Definition:** Poverty Reduction is the process utilized to identify the root causes of poverty and to promote community environments where individuals are able to lift themselves out of poverty.

> **Challenges/Issues:** According to the official measure from the US Census Bureau, Tucson's poverty rate as of 2012 was the sixth highest among large metropolitan statistical areas (MSAs) in the United States. Poverty in Tucson is highest among women, children, female-headed households where no husband is present, individuals living in non-family households, Native Americans, Hispanics, those with less than a high school degree, the foreign-born, and persons who aren't employed or who work less than full-time year-round. Of the census tracts that are fully or mostly within the City of Tucson, 15 had poverty rates above 40% between 2008 and 2012. There are identifiable census tracts where poverty is particularly acute. In our city, one is at the northeastern city limits, one to the east, three in the south, and the remaining ten neighborhoods contiguously spanning downtown, the university area, and north of the university up Miracle Mile. One quarter of Tucson's poor live in these 15 census tract neighborhoods, characterized by concentrated poverty.

> **4Tucson Goal:** Tucson residents successfully: 1) graduate high school, 2) secure employment, and 3) wait to have children until after marriage.

Our Poverty Reduction Research report is more than 100 pages. We shared the Poverty Reduction Taskforce Report with the Governor of our state, the Mayor of our city, the City Council, the County Board of Supervisors, the United Way and the Catholic Dioceses. You may download it from our website at 4Tucson.com.

Since our report was distributed, the conversation in Tucson has changed from the topic of homelessness to poverty reduction. That is just one indication that we are making an impact by identifying a key problem, quantifying it, and contributing to its understanding. Time will tell if our strategy will move Tucson from the sixth most impoverished city our size to something better. I believe it will.

Tony started taking our staff through the book of Nehemiah to help us identify city transformational principles that were transferable to building our product. The equivalent of Nehemiah's walls in Tucson are the structures and institutions of our city. The breaches in the walls of our city are just as visible as the breaches in the walls of Jerusalem and equally destructive to the peace and prosperity of our citizens. To use the imagery from the book of Nehemiah, we ask people to imagine Tucson without the protection of structures and institutions that provided the rules of law and the benefits of a shared cultural order that were intended to bring stability and prosperity.

City of Jerusalem
(during Nehemiah's Time)

Photo credit kzlam36.wordpress.com

In Nehemiah 1:4, he documents his strategy beginning with having a genuine concern for the ruins of the city. Nehemiah says: When I heard these words I sat down and wept, and mourned for days; and I continued fasting and praying before the God of heaven (RSV).

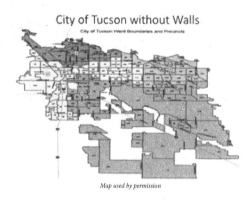

City of Tucson without Walls
City of Tucson Ward Boundaries and Precincts

Map used by permission

"We will not be able to build the walls of our city until we have first become greatly concerned about the ruins," Tony said.

- Have you taken the time to consider the ruins (what is broken) in your city?
- Have you thought about what your city could be under God as compared to what it is?
- Have you looked at your city's potential from a godly perspective to understand what it would take to reach that potential?

Like Nehemiah, you will need to open your eyes to the desolation and ruin in your city. You will need a heart that sincerely weeps and appeals to God out of concern for the devastation and suffering that ruin causes.

Nehemiah then engaged his heart when he saw the problems and he committed himself to do something about them. Look at chapter 1:11a.

Nehemiah prays:"O Lord, I pray, please let Your ear be attentive to the prayer of Your servant, and to the prayer of Your servants who desire to fear Your name; and let Your servant prosper this day, I pray…"

Even as Nehemiah is praying for his city, God begins developing a plan in his mind for rebuilding the walls. Nehemiah then asks God for something he needs to be successful. He prays, "…and grant me mercy in the sight of this man. For I was the king's cupbearer".

Out of concern for his city and after the confession of his heart, Nehemiah commits himself to the project. He asks God to begin moving in the heart of the man in authority over him to grant his request. In Nehemiah's case, it was the king.

How do we apply Nehemiah's story to our own? First, we become concerned for our city. Second, we confess our previous lack of concern. Third, we commit ourselves to take action. Fourth, we ask God to go before us, for invariably in a city enterprise like this, there will be factors in which we have no control. We must ask God for help and trust Him to orchestrate and arrange the factors that will ensure our success.

When Nehemiah began to implement his plan for reconstruction, he needed courage and a healthy respect for the opposition. In Chapter 2:9-10 we read, "Then I went to the governors in the region beyond the River, and gave them the king's letters. Now the king had sent captains of the army and horsemen with me. When Sanballat the Horonite and Tobiah the Ammonite official heard of it, they were deeply disturbed that a man had come to seek the well-being of the children of Israel."

The first thing Nehemiah faced when he arrived was the resistance. The guardians of the status quo. These are people who have a vested interest in keeping things the way they are. These people are not interested in the well-being of the city. They will resist the ways of God and will inevitably fight the work at every turn. They will be easily identifiable from the start, as they hear your plans to seek the peace and prosperity of your city. You will need courage to move forward in the face of opposition and the wisdom to avoid unnecessary clashes. Don't be surprised when you announce, "I will arise and build," that Satan will reply, "Then I will arise and oppose." Satan makes things difficult when we start turning the heart of the city back toward God.

The next six chapters of Nehemiah reveal the strategy of escalation the evil one will use as you begin working toward your goal. The strategies the guardians of the status quo will use to discourage you will be contempt, conspiracy, and cunning. The enemies of God will try to mock or heap contempt on what God is doing. When that fails, they will plot a conspiracy to overthrow the work. When that also fails, the opposition will escalate their efforts by devising a cunning scheme to distract or call you away from the work God has called you to do.

Another leadership step Nehemiah used was to remind the people to stay focused on where their blessings came from. He taught them how to continue in right relationship with God and how God wanted to use them to maintain the peace and prosperity of their city. Nehemiah 8:8 says, "So they read distinctly from the book, in the Law of God; and they gave the meaning, and helped them to understand the reading."

It is vitally important the people be taught to remain alert in maintaining the structures and institutions once they have been built. It is the structures and institutions that will provide the stability of the culture from one generation to the next. It is the legacy we leave to the next generation. It takes courage and a sound mind. Paul reminds Timothy of this very thing in 2 Timothy 1:6-7, "Therefore I remind you to stir up the gift of God which is in you through the laying on of my hands. For God has not given us a spirit of fear, but of power and of love and of a sound mind."

Biblical City Transformation is fragile. Maintaining what is important in your city will require continual effort. There will always be people who want to change things for their own benefit. The body of Christ must be reminded to stir up the gift of God which is in us, without fear, but in power and love and a sound mind to protect people from those who would take advantage of them. The best defense is a good offense. Keep identifying areas where the structures and institutions are misaligned and work to continually bring them into alignment. That is a lifetime project that requires diligence.

Sustainable Biblical City Transformation is our product. City transformation happens when the walls and gates provide peace and safety to all within its boundaries. Here is a diagram Tony created to help our partners visually see how the 22 city-wide Areas of Focus will serve to protect the families of our city and preserve the things they work hard for.

City of Tucson with Walls

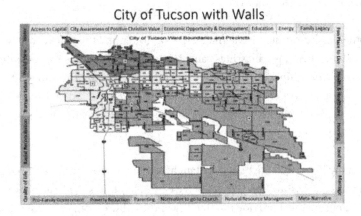

When the 22 Key Areas of Focus are secure, they will provide our citizens the opportunity to thrive in a city that encourages them to reach their God-given potential.

CHAPTER 12

Where to Start Your City Transformation Adventure

For I know the thoughts that I think toward you, says the LORD, thoughts of peace and not of evil, to give you a future and a hope. Then you will call upon Me and go and pray to Me, and I will listen to you. And you will seek Me and find Me, when you search for Me with all your heart.
Jeremiah 29:11-13

You need to understand, before you do anything else, that City Transformation is God's thing, not yours! It is one more way God can demonstrate His power through His body of believers so everyone in the city will recognize who He is. Before you start, would you seriously consider the answers to a few preparatory questions?

1. **Are you willing to follow God's lead and be obedient to what He tells you to do?**
    City Transformation occurs in proportion to our willingness to be used by God for His purposes and be obedient to what He calls you to do. God uses people as part of His divine plan for cities. The city of Nineveh would not have been transformed if Jonah had not been willing to be used by God for that purpose. The city of Jerusalem would not have been transformed if it were not for the obedience of Nehemiah to be used by God for that purpose.

2. **Are you willing to be used by God for His purpose in your city?**

One of the parables Jesus shared in the book of Luke serves as a great starting point for anyone contemplating leading a City Transformation movement. It is found in chapter 14, verses 26-30. It says, *"If anyone comes to Me and does not hate his father and mother, wife and children, brothers and sisters, yes, and his own life also, he cannot be My disciple. And whoever does not bear his cross and come after Me cannot be My disciple. For which of you, intending to build a tower, does not sit down first and count the cost, whether he has enough to finish it — lest, after he has laid the foundation, and is not able to finish, all who see it begin to mock him, saying, 'This man began to build and was not able to finish'."*

The purpose for leading a City Transformation movement is to bring God glory. The last thing you want is to be mocked for not counting the cost and determining whether you have what it takes to finish what you started. Calculating whether you have enough to complete the task of City Transformation, I believe, has to do more with your personal preparation and self-awareness than financial resources. Paul said, *"For I say, through the grace given to me, to everyone who is among you, not to think of himself more highly than he ought to think, but to think soberly, as God has dealt to each one a measure of faith (Romans 12:3).*

3. **How well have you prepared yourself for the journey?**
    Another point to consider before you start your adventure is your ability to work with other believers. Proverbs 11:14 says, *"Where there is no counsel, the people fall; but in the multitude of counselors there is safety."* Your probability for success is very low if you try doing this alone. Working with others will be the most fun thing you do and it will be the most frustrating. At times you will get the distinct feeling that City Transformation has more to do with maturing you as an individual than actually transforming the city. God could transform the city in a blink of an eye, but He has chosen to work through His followers — not just for the benefit of the city, but for our personal spiritual benefit. Working with

other believers will certainly humble you. Don't fight it — go with it. It is one of God's gifts to you. *"And he said to him, 'Well done, good servant; because you were faithful in a very little, have authority over ten cities'."* *(Luke 19:17)*

4. **How well do you play with other citizens of the kingdom of God?**
Let's look deeper into each of these preparation questions:

a. **Are you willing to follow God's lead and be obedient to what He tells you to do?**
Most Christian leaders will answer this question with a resounding, "Yes!" Jesus asked His disciples to pray with Him but found them asleep. He said, *"Watch and pray, lest you enter into temptation. The spirit indeed is willing, but the flesh is weak"* *(Matthew 26:41).*

If you are not careful when you start down this road, you may be tempted to make a poor choice at a time of great vulnerability and blow yourself up with an affair, or take money that does not belong to you or become filled with pride. To guard against these and other temptations, stay close to Jesus. Jesus said, *"Abide in Me, and I in you. As the branch cannot bear fruit of itself, unless it abides in the vine, neither can you, unless you abide in Me. I am the vine, you are the branches. He who abides in Me, and I in him, bears much fruit; for without Me you can do nothing"* *(John 15:4-5).*

To truly follow and be obedient to God's leadership you will need to develop strong personal, Christian disciplines in your life. It will be important to spend time daily in God's word and in prayer. Prayer is not just talking to God, but listening to what He tells you to do. It is also critical that you dedicate your time, talent, and treasure to His service. You are not your own, you were bought with a price. Consider the importance of 2 Timothy 2:4. It will be important for you to learn how to build effective relationships with believers and with unbelievers. Without these disciplines in your life, it will be next to impossible to obediently follow God's leadership. The less disciplined you are in any one of these areas decreases the probability that you will successfully lead a City Transformation movement.

b. Are you willing to be used by God for His purpose in your city?
So many times our prayers are about our desires and what we want God to do for us. To be a good city leader, that must be reversed. He does not serve you, you serve Him. Our prayer lives must be about God's desires and what He wants to do through us. Matthew 6:31-34 is one of my favorite passages that helps keep me balanced. It says, *"Therefore do not worry, saying, 'What shall we eat?' or 'What shall we drink?' or 'What shall we wear?' For after all these things the Gentiles seek. For your heavenly Father knows that you need all these things. But seek first the kingdom of God and His righteousness, and all these things shall be added to you. Therefore, do not worry about tomorrow, for tomorrow will worry about its own things. Sufficient for the day is its own trouble."*

You must be committed to what God wants more than what you want. You must be willing to be poured out as an offering for God's purpose for the benefit of your city. *"Do all things without complaining and disputing, that you may become blameless and harmless, children of God without fault in the midst of a crooked and perverse generation, among whom you shine as lights in the world holding fast the word of life, so that I may rejoice in the day of Christ that I have not run in vain or labored in vain. Yes, and if I am being poured out as a drink offering on the sacrifice and service of your faith, I am glad and rejoice with you all"* (Philippians 2:14-17).

c. How well have you prepared yourself for the journey?
In the New Living Translation, Romans 12:3 says, *"Because of the privilege and authority God has given me, I give each of you this warning: Don't think you are better than you really are. Be honest in your evaluation of yourselves, measuring yourselves by the faith God has given us."*

Being a city leader that people look to for spiritual guidance and direction can be intimidating. It is wise to take time to know how God made you — both strengths and weaknesses. God has made you with some incredibly wonderful strengths and talents, but He did not give you everything you need to succeed in what He has called you to do. You will need other believers to work with you who are equally gifted, but in different ways. You will need to trust them as much as you desire them to trust you.

To get a better understanding of the gifts and talents you bring to the table, it might be helpful to do a few personal assessments. There are many good spiritual gifts indicators. Find one that you like. Some assessments I have found most helpful are: Myers-Briggs Type Indicator, a personality indicator; StrengthsFinder, a talents indicator; and Hershey Blanchard Situational Leadership Style, a leadership-style indicator. There are other good tools for self-assessment, but these have helped me the most.

Once you understand and embrace the fact God created you for City Transformation and He created others who will want to join you who are equally gifted, you will be less intimidated by high capacity people on your team. Be faithful to who you are and do what you are good at. Trust God to bring others who are good at the things you are not and trust them to do what He has called them to do. It is easy to say, not easy to do.

d. How well do you play with other citizens of the kingdom of God?
Christians are notorious for living and working in silos. Patrick Lencioni
in his book, *Silos, Politics and Turf Wars* (Jossey-Bass, 2006) says, "*Silos
are nothing more than the barriers that exist between departments within
an organization, causing people who are supposed to be on the same team
to work against one another.*"

Christians who are, in fact, on the same team, God's team, often isolate
themselves by denomination, race, culture, socio-economic status, and
geography. If not one of these reasons, Christians will find almost any
other reason to silo and work against people on the same team. The key
to City Transformation is to keep your eye on the big picture. The big
picture is that the kingdom of God involves a lot of Jesus followers who
may not be your particular brand or denomination, may not be your
color, or live in your part of town, but who are all committed to following
Jesus and making a difference with their lives. You will naturally like
some more than others, but you are responsible for working in unity with
them all.

Do you remember what Jesus told his disciples in Mark 9:38-40? "*John
said to Jesus, 'Teacher, we saw someone using your name to cast out
demons, but we told him to stop because he wasn't in our group.' 'Don't stop
him!' Jesus said. 'No one who performs a miracle in my name will soon be
able to speak evil of me. Anyone who is not against us is for us.*'" (NLT)

Paul put it this way in his letter to the Philippians. Starting in chapter 1
verses 15-18, "*Some indeed preach Christ even from envy and strife, and
some also from goodwill: The former preach Christ from selfish ambition,
not sincerely, supposing to add affliction to my chains; but the latter out of
love, knowing that I am appointed for the defense of the gospel. What then?
Only that in every way, whether in pretense or in truth, Christ is preached;
and in this I rejoice, yes, and will rejoice.*"

I am not saying that we embrace heresy. What I am saying is there are a lot of Christians, from a lot of churches in your city, who you do not know yet but will be in heaven right beside you. It might be a good idea to get to know them while you are on this earth and work together with them serving as ambassadors for the same King. Working together for the common good of a city will not happen without Christians intentionally working at it. That is God's design for the city and for you.

Maybe learning to work together for a common goal was the intent behind the last prayer Jesus prayed before going to the cross. It is found in John 17. We will start with verse 15, Jesus prayed, *"I do not pray that You should take them out of the world, but that You should keep them from the evil one. They are not of the world, just as I am not of the world. Sanctify them by Your truth. Your word is truth. As You sent Me into the world, I also have sent them into the world. And for their sakes I sanctify Myself, that they also may be sanctified by the truth. I do not pray for these alone, but also for those who will believe in Me through their word; that they all may be one, as You, Father, are in Me, and I in You; that they also may be one in Us, that the world may believe that You sent Me. And the glory which You gave Me I have given them, that they may be one just as We are one: I in them, and You in Me; that they may be made perfect in one, and that the world may know that You have sent Me, and have loved them as You have loved Me"* (emphasis added).

The Holy Spirit continues to intercede for us. Jesus knew that it would be our natural tendency to silo. He prayed that we would learn to work together for the Kingdom in unity as proof that the Father sent Him.

The Holy Spirit is working within our hearts, helping us learn to play well with each other as evidence that Jesus is who He says He is. We at 4Tucson are praying and believing that the Christians in our city will become the answer to the prayer Jesus prayed in John 17.

CHAPTER 13
Funding Strategies

But seek first the kingdom of God and His righteousness, and all these things shall be added to you. Therefore, do not worry about tomorrow, for tomorrow will worry about its own things. Sufficient for the day is its own trouble.

Matthew 6:33-34

Before asking, "How do I fund my City Transformation movement?" it might serve you to ask a different question: "What is the desired outcome of my city transformational model?" If you start with the wrong question, you may end up in the wrong place. In other words, if you don't know where you are going, any method will get you there. You need to hear from God to know the way. Psalm 143:8 is a wonderful reminder of that. *"Cause me to hear Your lovingkindness in the morning, for in You do I trust; cause me to know the way in which I should walk, for I lift up my soul to You."*

The Vision of 4Tucson is to serve as a catalyst to engage the Christian community in bringing about spiritual and societal transformation for the benefit of the whole city.

We believe God has given us this vision. Raising funds for it has been a challenge from the beginning. We have tried a lot of fundraising strategies and have witnessed a wide range of results. Not always what we expected. If we are going to be successful in achieving the vision God has given us, the question then became, "How will God provide the resources to do it?"

Reviewing data from the City of Tucson website, we get a glimpse of how the cultural history of our city will impact our fundraising. *"For over 200 centuries, Tucson was home solely to Native Americans. It was then the Frontera del Norte of New Spain for about 40 years, then part of the Republic of Mexico for about 30 years. In 1854, Tucson became part of the United States with the Gadsden Purchase (Treaty of Mesilla)."* As a result, *"In 2000, Tucson had the 8th largest city in number of Native Americans. In 1990, the metro area was 23rd largest in number of Hispanics."* Just as the diversity of Tucson's history impacts the methodology we use in our fundraising, the demographics of the city should also be considered when creating your city fundraising strategies.

In 2000, the racial/ethnic breakdown of Metro Tucson (Pima County) was:
- 61.48% White, Non-Hispanic, alone
- 29.34% Hispanic (can be any race)
- 2.85% Black/African American, alone
- 2.59% Native American, alone
- 1.97% Asian, alone
- 0.11% Native Hawaiian or Pacific Islander, alone
- 0.12% Other, alone (self-identified)
- 1.55% Two or more races

The cultural and demographic makeup of your city will determine which funding strategies are likely to have the highest probability of success. Tucson has more recent statistics than those shared here, but the ebbs and flows of the population have little impact on the next point I want to illustrate. The cultural and demographic makeup of your city matters when it comes to fundraising strategies.

Tucson is 61% white, therefore our most successful fundraising strategy for our white staff members has been the **Personal Missionary Support Model** used by many ministries such as CRU, Navigators, and Intervarsity. It is culturally accepted in the traditional white church for missionaries to ask church members for missionary support.

There are two additional fundraising models that we have used successfully within a white cultural context. They have served us well in the early stages of developing our model. They are:

1. **High Capacity Pastor/Staff Model:** This method involves a pastor or designated staff member to be released by the church to give 20% or more of his time to city-reaching.

    The Oasis Church has been very gracious in allowing me to give more than 50% of my time as the Executive Director of 4Tucson while at the same time serving fulltime as their Senior Pastor. Our church has a dedicated Associate Pastor, Dennis Watson, and Women's and Children's Director, Pam Hayes, who handle the administrative details of our church programs and fill the gap I leave to be able to love on our people. Without the full commitment to City Transformation by the church and the staff, I would not have been able to give so much of my time to developing 4Tucson.

2. **Patron Model:** In this model, one or two large donors/businesses/ministries provide salary and organizational support for a designated period of time.

    We were blessed in the early stages of our development to have a businessman come along side us, who had a passion to see our city changed. He understood the potential impact our model could have on changing the city. He committed to invest one million dollars over a five-year period. His gift was front-loaded. He understood that to start something required more money up front. He set up a schedule, giving us more money for the start-up and decreasing his investment 20% each year thereafter. His desire was to help us get the model operational and to achieve success on our own without building dependency. He said, *"I am willing to help with the start-up costs, but for this model to be effective, God is going to have to bring other investors who catch the dream of what we are doing, recognize the early results from the first few years, and then be willing themselves to invest financially to see the plan to its completion."*

Matching Funds is another tool for a patron to use to leverage their impact and to encourage additional buy-in from other Christian investors.

3. **Kingdom Business Model: The theory with this model is for a business to be created for the primary purpose of using the profits to fund ministry.**

I personally started a business with the specific purpose of using the profits to fund church planting. One of the strengths I have is that I am good at business. God created me with a knack for starting businesses and making money through them. Because of my entrepreneurial background, starting a business seemed like a good fundraising strategy. Because I preached on weekends and had limited time to create something from the ground up, I purchased a franchise. With a franchise, you can be up and running in a relatively short period of time. For the first several years the business provided the financial resources we needed to fund church planting. When the economy collapsed, so did my business. My brilliant business fundraising strategy started to consume a lot of time and money just to keep the doors open. The money available for ministry stopped abruptly.

Another advantage of the Kingdom Business model is that it created jobs for many people over the years. The business provided a quality, needed service in the community and allowed the business to provide marketable skills for entry- level job seekers. This model also put me in contact with many business owners and city leaders I would not have met otherwise. From experience, I acknowledge this model does have its risks. In the right situation, it might be a good model for those with an entrepreneur bent.

Jim Weisert and I have started another business together with the purpose of funding 4Tucson. Our business model is to purchase local, distressed businesses with the intent of keeping them in Tucson and keeping their employees employed. Our strategy is to turn the business around, locate a potential owner operator and sell the business within five years. We agreed to use half of the profit to fund 4Tucson and half to purchase more businesses. The business is just getting started, so we can't share if it works or not.

As you can see, no one fundraising method worked for us. It was a combination of several strategies. I cannot overstate how the generosity of my church, the dedication of my church staff, and the generosity of godly business leaders were key to launching 4Tucson. Looking in from the perspective of an insider, it has been remarkable how God brought all the right people and the right combination of financial resources together in just the right way. It serves to encourage us that God is leading us.

We shared our experience using several models for fundraising with our minority city leaders who wanted to serve through 4Tucson. We trained them how to raise funds for their salary support. After several unsuccessful attempts applying one or more of these models, we had to face the reality that what worked in a white context was woefully inadequate in a minority context. The Pew Research Center published a study in 2011 entitled, _Wealth Gaps Rise to Record Highs Between White, Blacks, Hispanics_. The report analyzed census data and found that *"the median wealth of white households is 20 times that of black households and 18 times that of Hispanic households."* In real numbers that means *"…the typical black household had just $5,677 in wealth (assets minus debts); the typical Hispanic household had $6,325 in wealth; and the typical white household had $113,149."*

When white people ask other white people for financial support, it is more likely than not if the missionary keeps at it, he or she will reach their fundraising goal. It has been our experience at 4Tucson, that the results of that strategy are dramatically less successful for our black and Hispanic staff members. Minority missionaries do not have the same social capital or cultural context to raise money the way white missionaries do.

The information revealed to us was that if 4Tucson is to achieve its vision of spiritual and societal transformation for the whole city, we would also need to have city missionaries representing the diversity of the whole city. We have found that it is one thing for Christians from various ethnic groups to partner together on a short-term city-wide project. It is an entirely different story when we ask them to invest their money to ensure that the diversity of the city is represented on our staff.

Samuel Perry, a Dallas Theological Seminary graduate and Ph.D. candidate in Sociology at the University of Chicago, published an article in 2011: *Diversity, Donations, and Disadvantage: The Implications of Personal Fundraising for Racial Diversity in Evangelical Outreach Ministries.* In his research, he found *"for objective fundraising outcomes, the odds of raising one's full support were 66% lower for African Americans and Latinos relative to whites…[and] the odds that they had to pick up a second job to supplement their income were twice that of white staff."*

We learned through experience that the traditional models white missionaries use to raise funds does not work well for minority missionary staff. When it does work, it is the exception rather than the rule.

With 39% of Tucson's population representing minorities, we discovered rather quickly that different fundraising models had to be explored to raise financial support for our minority staff. I would not say we have this figured out, but here are a couple ideas we are working on to raise financial support for our minority staff members.

Cross-Cultural Missionary Experience:
One of the fundraising ideas 4Tucson is exploring with my friend, Angel Morfin, a Hispanic pastor on our staff, is to leverage his cultural context. Anglo upper-income Christians often pay $1000 or more per person for an adventure and thrill seeking trip. It is not uncommon for them to pay $5000 or more per person to go on a missions trip to a foreign country. It occurred to us that Anglo Christians might be willing to pay for Cross-Cultural Missionary Experiences right in our own city. The idea is to create opportunities for affluent Anglo groups to come together for a weekend cross-cultural experience where they are able to witness God at work in the city firsthand. Group members would pay for the experience and in return receive cross-cultural training, participate in a cross-culture community project, and take part in a cross-culture worship experience with a traditional meal prepared by the minority group with whom they spent their weekend. The groups do not have to leave town to have a mountain top spiritual experience. The seeds for long-term relationships are sown through the mutual experience and the proceeds from the weekend financially support the minority staff member.

Generosity Model
My friend Jim and I have had the privilege of facilitating several Journey of Generosity Retreats with affluent people in our city. The retreat materials are provided free of charge to participants through the generosity of the Maclellan Foundation and Generous Giving. One of the videos shown at the retreat is the Handful of Rice.

We learned that teaching biblical principles of generosity allowed some of the poorest communities in the world to become creatively self-supporting. We are experimenting with this model in our city. We are trying to work collaboratively with the poorer communities to help them fund a city missionary to 4Tucson. This is still in the early development phase and therefore has not proven to work in our context. We believe by teaching the principles of generosity, this model offers good potential for people of every socio-economic level to be financially invested in city transformation.

Legacy Model
Young Life (a youth ministry organization) regions around the country are creating Legacy Funds for urban staff. In general, the Legacy Model is an endowment of $3 - 5 million used to assist the fund-raising efforts of minority staff. By partnering with them, Legacy Funds fill the gap between what minority staff members are able to personally raise and what they need to sustain their families.

At 4Tucson, we are working to create a similar fund that would work in a similar way as an endowed chair at a university. A percentage of our Domain Directors and Taskforce Directors are and will continue to be minorities. It has been our experience that our minority brothers and sisters serve as some of the best examples of Jesus followers and catalysts for city transformation. Because of difficulties they encountered raising salary support, some of minority staff members have not been able to take care of their families and continue to serve on our staff. We believe like most universities, that an endowment fund to help with salary support is crucial for recruiting and retaining the highest-quality people, the best minds, the most creative researchers, and the most engaged city changers regardless of ethnicity. At this time, we do not have an endowment fund, but we are working toward that goal, believing that it is part of the long-term fundraising strategy of 4Tucson.

Partnership (Membership) Model

Ultimately, we believe our Partnership Model will prove to be the key for our long-term sustainability. The Partnership Model involves partners or members. We chose to call them partners, because it implied serving as opposed to just belonging. A partner of 4Tucson is a Christian who agrees to follow a simple biblical Code of Ethics and gives a minimum of $10/month to 4Tucson. Businesses, churches and nonprofits may also become partners by giving $35/month.

Biblical City Transformation requires mobilization and engagement of Christians across our city. While our Partners give to the organization, they are not viewed as just a funding source but rather our most valuable asset. They work together with other Christians in specific areas of passion or expertise for long-term sustainable biblical city transformation. Our Partners are important because they are the ones who will be working to address our city's most difficult and systemic problems by implementing biblical solutions. They are the true city changers who invest their hearts into the city by giving both of their time and treasure. We are continually asking Christians to give their heart to the cause of city transformation. In both the gospels of Matthew and Luke, Jesus is quoted saying, *"For where your treasure is, there your heart will be also."* The $10 per month is not about the money. It is about the heart. We are recruiting Christians whose hearts are committed to God, committed to each other, and who are committed to serve with other Christians to transform our city in Jesus' name.

A partner's $10 a month gives every Christian an opportunity to invest in what God is doing in the city. Their monthly gift helps fill the gaps in raising salary support of our city missionaries. Our stated goal is to recruit 100,000 Christians across our city for Biblical City Transformation in Tucson. We are considering whether 100,000 Christians across the city giving $10/month may be how the Handful of Rice model works in our context. Whether or not it is, we believe the Partnership model is the key to our long-term fundraising strategy.

As we work toward our vision, we are experimenting with every creative fundraising method we can find until we reach our goal. There is no magic bullet for fundraising. As we have said repeatedly, it starts with a God-given vision for your city. I think I heard it first from Pastor Rick Warren that, *"money always follows vision."* Without a solid vision, you will not successfully raise money.

After you have a clear vision, it really comes down to faith and trusting God. Matthew 6:3 says, "seek first the Kingdom of God and His righteousness, and these other things [finances] will be added to us." He also tells us to *"ask, and it will be given to you; seek, and you will find; knock, and it will be opened to you" (Matthew 7:7).*

Other Resources for Fundraising:
Mission Increase Foundation has been very helpful to us. They come along side Christian ministries to help them discover biblical strategies and processes that, when followed, will fund their God-given vision and mission. They offer workshops, coaching, and consulting. Their training can cut years off of your learning curve for funding your city movement. I highly recommend taking their training and coaching — and it is free. You will discover they are a valuable tool for helping your organization wisely developing fundraising strategies. Here is a link to their website: www.mif.org.

National Christian Foundation (NCF) is another valuable resource. NCF is a non-profit organization that helps primarily Christian donors give more wisely and tax-efficiently to support their favorite charitable causes. NCF will help your donors with non-cash assets (for example stocks, real estate, and business interests) to create donor-advised funds that may help your organization. Here is a link to their website: www.ncfgiving.com.

Journey of Generosity (JOG) has a mission to spread the biblical message of generosity in order to grow generous givers among those entrusted with much. This is **not** a fundraising strategy!!! The weekend retreats serve to bless people who have the means to financially bless others in your city. It will challenge attendees to better understand what real biblical generosity looks like. It will be life changing for them. This retreat is not about getting something from large donors. It is about giving something to them. It is about blessing them. While attendees may expect it, there is no asking for money at these retreats. When enough people go through JOG, it will create a culture of generosity in your city. Here is a link to their website: www.generousgiving.org.

In Hebrews 11, the Bible says, *"Now faith is the substance of things hoped for, the evidence of things not seen…without faith it is impossible to please Him, for he who comes to God must believe that He is, and that He is a rewarder of those who diligently seek Him."*

It is important to count the cost of starting a City Transformation movement. It is equally important to be obedient to what God is calling you to do and not let money or the lack of it, determine your obedience. Pray for wisdom and discernment concerning your vision and your fundraising strategies. When you hear from God — go for it!

CONCLUSION
What Will History Say About Us?

One of my favorite scriptures is found in the book of Acts. It says in part, "For David, after he had served his own generation by the will of God, fell asleep, was buried with his fathers..."
(Acts 13:36).

Every successive generation faces significant threats that must be heroically addressed to prepare the way for the next generation. These threats may be geo-political, like wars; they may be financial, like the Great Depression; or they may be spiritual, like large numbers of people walking away from following God's ways. How those threats are addressed often defines that generation in the annals of history.

A popular term used recently is the "Greatest Generation." It refers to a generation that grew up during the Great Depression and then went on to fight in World War II. In his book by that title, Tom Brokaw wrote, *"It is, I believe, the greatest generation any society has ever produced."* He argued that these men and women fought not for fame and recognition, but because it was the *"right thing to do."* As King David, they served their own generation by the will of God and now most have been buried with their fathers. We remember that generation as the benefactors of the society we now enjoy.

When the Battle of Britain was about to begin, Winston Churchill said, *"Upon this battle depends the survival of Christian civilization."* I would propose that the greatest threat to our generation is that the institutions of our society:

the family, the church, and the schools are all under attack. These three institutions, more than any others, are responsible for preserving our society for the next generation.

As the threats to these three institutions intensifies, most Christians seem unaware that they are in a fight for the survival of their way of life. War is being waged threatening the very soul of our cities, states, and nation. Our Founding Fathers created a nation on the premise that its citizens could be self-governed, if it were built on the pillars of religion and morality. Our generation's greatest test will be passing on a healthy nation to the next generation with its foundations intact. Will history judge our generation as the one that allowed the institutional foundations that have preserved our nation for the last 240 years to crumble? It is essential for us to understand that without preserving the principles of Christianity, the next generation will likely disintegrate into a new dark age.

That is not what I want the history books to say about my generation. That is not the legacy I want to pass on to my kids. 4Tucson is our attempt to help Christians in our generation engage the culture and pass on a legacy we would be proud of. Will you join us in building a city and a nation the next generation will thank us for? Please join other Christians working toward that end by using what we have learned. Our City Transformation Model works. Together we can make history in every city in America that will make our children proud.

APPENDIX A
2016 Successes

Throughout 2016, 4Tucson staff, board members, and volunteers continued to develop the City Transformation strategy and communicate our progress to our partners in the community. There are many evidences of God working through us in both Domains and Taskforces. Here are a few examples we are able to share with you.

Church Domain
David Drum, Director

- Through alliances such as the Pastor's Partnership, pastors and church members across races and denominations are uniting for events like: Worship Over Tucson, March for Jesus, Love Conquers Hate, Love Conquers Racism, and the annual Easter Sunrise Service, hosted by the Interdenominational Ministerial Alliance (IMA), a group of African-American pastors seeking unity across denominations. Jesus' prayer in John 17 is being answered!

- For years, pastors coming out of the three-day Pastor Prayer Summits have asked, "How can we help our congregational members experience the same citywide unity we're blessed with as pastors?" The John 17 Weekends, new in 2016, are one answer. On separate weekends, 70 men and 70 women experienced 72 hours together in an intense Christian retreat focused on the gospel of Jesus Christ, our citywide unity, and training in how to impact our environments as Christians. The response has been phenomenal, with tremendous enthusiasm already building for the 2017 weekends.

- With a monthly attendance of 60-120 participants, the Tucson Ministry Alliance (TMA), a collaborative effort from multiple organizations such as Community Renewal and 4Tucson, has promoted unity across congregational lines. TMA just completed its fifth year with consistent positive feedback and impact. The Hispanic TMA, which was launched in early 2016, has reached approximately 20 regular attendees, focusing on unity among pastors of different Spanish-speaking congregations.

Education Domain
Bernadette Gruber, director

- Celebrating its second baccalaureate service for seniors graduating from high school, the Education Domain continues to encourage students from public schools with a ceremony of faith and blessing.

- There are now more than 150 church-school partnerships, serving eight school districts in the Tucson area. This means over 80% of schools in Tucson have a church-school partnership. The Education Domain has been instrumental in training, equipping, and mobilizing the Christian community to engage in these church-school partnerships. Churches have been able to bless students, faculty and staff through projects including: campus beautification, tutoring programs, teacher appreciation, mentoring programs, school supply donations, weekend food packs, family food boxes, and more. In addition, five school districts regularly hold religious leader gatherings to further these relationships in their districts.

- The Education Domain, in conjunction with the TUSD Student Equity Department, hosted its second TUSD Pastor Appreciation Breakfast attended by 100 pastors, ministry leaders and district administrators. Powerful testimonies were shared illustrating how beneficial these church-school partnerships are to the schools and community. These TUSD pastor appreciation gatherings have led to further collaboration with schools and churches.

Environment Domain
Dan Porzio, Director

- The Environment Domain is in its early stages of development. Director, Dan Porzio, has researched water use and solar power conservation and other environmental concerns on both a state and regional level, identifying all the stakeholders engaged in conservation/use issues. Porzio is preparing preliminary reports on his research, which will be used to direct the next steps for the Environment Domain and future taskforces.

Government Domain
Paul Parisi, Director

- Raising awareness across the city, the Government Domain has facilitated Constitution Classes in both English and Spanish. More than 300 people completed classes in English and 75 people completed them in Spanish.

- Director, Paul Parisi, traveled weekly to the Arizona State Capitol to participate in meetings as a member of the Arizona Values Action Team, chaired by Center for Arizona Policy President, Cathi Herrod, and State Senator, Steve Yarbrough. The mission of AVAT is to advance public policy that is pro-life, pro-traditional marriage, pro-school choice and pro-religious freedom. Many legislators and other like-minded stakeholder organizations attended these meetings, creating an environment in which to strengthen relationships and develop new partnerships.

- During the fall 2016 elections, the Government Domain successfully advocated for, or against, several ballot initiatives that impacted the well-being of the Tucson community.

Justice Domain
Da-Mond Holt, former Director

- The Expungement Workshop Program began in April, 2016. This program assisted non-violent ex-offenders in cleaning up their backgrounds by getting their convictions set aside, and helped them secure employment, housing and basic support.

- On "Warrant Day," the City of Tucson opened its court building giving people a weekend day to clear up outstanding warrants. Through this domain's partnership with the Superior Court, 249 people had outstanding arrest warrants resolved.

- The Justice Forum had a great turnout with a strong, diverse panel and 85 attendees. Former Director, Da'Mond Holt, received positive feedback, saying that a forum is exactly what the community needs.

Philanthropy Domain
Linda Goode, Director

- The first Philanthropy Fellowship luncheon launched in early 2016 and was a success with 34 registrants, leading to new partnerships.

The theme was "Moving Tucsonans from Poverty to Stability to Generosity." Guest speakers included Rosalva Zimmerman from the Department of Economic Security in Tucson, and Judy Davidson and Becky Nissen, founders of Kingdom Investment Foundation based here in Tucson.

- The Philanthropy Domain just launched a new Kingdom Advisors Fellowship for professionals who help others manage their financial resources and who are interested in incorporating their faith with their practice. A number of financial professionals have expressed interest in being involved. This fellowship will continue to meet the second Friday of each month in 2017.

- This domain also hosted Family Budgeting and Money Management classes at several locations.

Prayer Domain
Brian Goodall, Director

- Fervent in belief about the power of prayer, Director Brian Goodall helped partner with Arizona National Day of Prayer, to organize and promote a citywide event on National Day of Prayer. This event, held at the Tucson Convention Center, was attended by over 3,000 people. At this gathering, 4Tucson presented the first 30-minute documentary film on Tucson's spiritual heritage, celebrating how people have responded to God's leadership in our city's past and encouraging Christians to discover their part in Tucson's future. Many made the pledge to pray daily for Tucson and now join hundreds of others in that commitment.

- The Prayer Domain also organized a special Art Gallery event, commissioning over 20 local artists to create diverse expressions of prayer for Tucson's future, inspired by stories from our city's spiritual heritage. The exhibit also featured original DeGrazia paintings depicting the life of Father Kino from Ted DeGrazia's personal collection. In addition, included in the gallery was a huge collage of coloring pages produced by elementary-aged kids from Vineyard Christian Community and Pantano Christian Church, sharing how they believe God wants to use them to bless people they know in Tucson. Their works included their own personal prayer for our city.

- City Psalms completed their second album of songs of prayer for Tucson, written and recorded by local worship leaders and Christian musicians. The studio producer told Goodall he thinks this is one of the most high-quality, well thought-out, creative and original albums he has heard come out of Tucson. High praise! Watch for the album release in 2017!

Social Services Domain
J. Michael Davis, Director

- CarePortal in Tucson celebrated its one-year anniversary on December 3, 2016. Through CarePortal, a partnership between 4Tucson, the Department of Child Safety (DCS) and churches, the lives of over 850 children and 350 families were impacted in 2016. CarePortal helps keep children who are not being abused or neglected out of the foster care system and in their homes, by helping to meet basic needs of families, such as fire extinguishers, plumbing etc. The church steps in to meet these needs.

Through 4Tucson's encouragement and promotion, the city, and now state, has 43 churches partnering with DCS via CarePortal, and

16 more are seriously considering joining. Even the Governor has noted that CarePortal played a role in keeping the percentage of kids entering the Foster Care System in Pima County steady, rather than increasing each year like other counties in Arizona (for example, rates increased by 20% in Maricopa County). Based on this, the Governor recently initiated CarePortal in Maricopa County as well.

In 2017, we will be initiating the Tier 2 level of CarePortal, a move for churches to reach more than just physical needs of families (as in Tier 1) and extend to meet interpersonal needs, providing support for families desperate to stay together.

Sports Domain
Ed Noble, Director

- The 4Tucson Sports Domain held several events in 2016 that helped bring people together in fellowship. 4Tucson hosted the Triple Play, which included Bowling 4Tucson, the ForeTucson Golf Tournament and a Diamondbacks game. These were fun events, bringing together many of our faithful partners, as well as new friends. From getting out of the heat to go bowling at LuckyStrike, to traveling to Chase Field for a special Diamondbacks game called 'Faith and Family Night,' the Sports Domain offered a lot of great opportunities to be involved. Each event began with prayer, giving thanks to the Lord for all He provides, and was an opportunity to be a witness to other attendees at these events. For example, 70 golfers gathering in prayer before descending out onto the Del Lago golf course was a powerful witness—a sight to behold!

Media and Arts Domain
Angelina Hannum, Director

- A new domain director was successfully hired for the Media and Arts Domain and will be starting in January, 2017. We welcome Angelina Hannum to 4Tucson and look forward to the development of this domain under her leadership!

- 4Tucson continues participation in the Tucson Worship Conference, an event held annually to help train and encourage local worship teams across our city.

Poverty Reduction Taskforce
Barbara Jimenez, Chair

- Created a research report of the issue of poverty in Tucson.

- Distributed the report to key leaders in the city.

- Formed the first Taskforce team and created a biblically based Action Plan.

- Created Transformation Teams to implement the Action Plan.

Concluding Summary

Overall, 4Tucson has seen remarkable evidence that the City Transformation Model is God's strategy for renewing Tucson. 4Tucson has found great favor from the Governor's office to local school boards. Collaborative partnerships that were unthinkable three years ago are now a reality, as we continue to connect Christians who have a heart for this city.

Signs of 4Tucson making a difference comes in the form of a note in TUSD's community e-newsletter. It reads: *"Thank you to our supporters in the faith-based community. From free tutoring to weekend food backpacks and mentoring programs, these volunteers are making a difference every day and we thank them!"*

The year 2016 was a year of incredible blessing and accomplishment—a year of reaffirming direction and assessing how best to move forward. 4Tucson continues our commitment to serving as a catalyst for biblical change that helps the most people possible. We are excited to see what God does through us in 2017!

APPENDIX B
Focus Area Definitions, Challenges, and Goals

Moral and Cultural Heritage

Each culture determines its own morals, usually derived from a plurality of people in that culture. That culture's ethics are usually derived from the beliefs which rest outside of the perception or acknowledgement of a given culture. Cultural Heritage is the legacy of physical and intangible attributes of a society that are inherited from past generations, maintained in the present and bestowed for the benefit of future generations.

1. **Worldview**

    Definition: A worldview is the set of truth claims that every individual uses to frame a comprehensive understanding of life. As Christians we derive our understanding of life from the Bible.

    Challenges/Issues: There are multiple worldviews in our society (each one based on various platforms of knowledge acquisition or generation — inclusive of tradition, intuition, research, faith, etc.). Each worldview asserts its own claim to truth.

    4Tucson Goal: The Citizens of Tucson will value the biblical perspective and make decisions collectively and individually from a biblical point of view.

2. **Meta-Narrative**

    Definition: A meta-narrative is a big-picture view. The Bible declares that there is an over-arching story of God's purposeful plan for humanity and a specific call for His people to participate in that plan.

Challenges/Issues: A meta-narrative is the "Big Story," that serves as an explanation for the many little stories in a culture. The meta-narrative of the Bible is God revealing Himself to mankind and His call to each individual to participate in God's story (Eph 2:10). Postmodern thought does not believe in meta-narratives and teach that there are no grand stories which give meaning to all of life and which define what is true. This leads to despair and hopelessness in a culture.

4Tucson Goal: Citizens of Tucson accepting their individual role in God's bigger story.

3. **City Awareness of Positive Christian Values**
   Definition: City awareness of positive Christian value is the condition whereby city leaders and residents are aware of the Christian community's value system and the standards that are used as the basis for ethical and moral achievements.

   Challenges/Issues: The values communicated by modern culture are often in direct opposition to the teachings of Christianity. Christian values are often demeaned by people in authority equating them with fables or myths. Understanding Christian values and concepts are key to a healthy society.

   4Tucson Goal: 51% of citizens embracing and promoting shared values derived from a love for God and a love for our neighbors will have a positive effect on the city as a whole.

4. **Normative to go to Church**
   Definition: Normative to go to church is the behavioral pattern whereby the majority of citizens within a community regularly attend church. Churches form a visible sign in the world of the invisible reality of the

kingdom of God. Christians are commanded in Hebrews 10:24-25 to stir up love, good works, and to assemble together.

Challenges/Issues: Church attendance is one best measures of spiritual health of a city. Understanding the Bible is critical to understanding America's form of government. Church attendees are also the best source of engaged volunteers in the city. It has been found that 53% of church attendees volunteer as compared to 19% of non-church goers. Churches provide a vital safety net for providing critical services to the most vulnerable in our society. More than 70% of Tucson's population state they are Christians, but only 8% of its residents attend church on a regular basis. Church attendance is in decline in America and therefore the influence of Christianity on culture (salt and light) is fading.

4Tucson Goal: 51% of Tucson citizenry attending weekly church services.

5. **Racial Reconciliation**
   Definition: Racial Reconciliation is the act of people of various races who were once at enmity with or unaware of one another, moving to a state of friendly relations.

   Challenges/Issues: People within Tucson continue to be divided along racial and ethnic lines. Issues of education, unemployment, poverty, equality, and shared values remain points of division. Sunday continues to be the most segregated time of the week for residents.

   4Tucson Goal: Bring the strengths of all races to work together for the mutual success of Tucson's citizens.

6. **Pro-family Government**
   Definition: A pro-family government is a government that favors, supports, encourages and promotes traditional family structures and values through policy and laws.

Challenges/Issues: Federal, state, and local governments have the legal authority (constitutional right) to develop and pass laws (U.S. Constitution, Arizona Constitution, Arizona Revised Statues, City of Tucson Ordinances, etc.) that govern its citizenry. Anti-family provisions may arise out of state, county, and city governments if the people (voters) are not engaged in issues.

4Tucson Goal: A supportive government allowing citizens to make choices for their family unit.

Community and Family Stability

A community's stability can be measured by the overall spiritual, psychological, emotional, and physical health of the majority of its citizens. Research shows that the health of a person is formed very early in life by factors such as their biological makeup, familial relationships, social interactions, and physical environment. As young people mature into adults they engage in marriage, have children, and work to achieve a quality of life that has personal satisfaction.

1. **Marriage**

   Definition: Marriage is the legal union of a man and a woman being recognized as husband and wife by spiritual, social, and government institutions.

   Challenges/Issues: There is ample evidence to support the concept that committed and stable relationships have a positive effect on the married couple, their children, and on society as a whole. A healthy family is a key determinant in a stable community. The family is the smallest unit designed by God to support health and sustainability in any community.

   4Tucson Goal: Making biblical marriage a valued asset for Tucson citizens.

2. **Parenting**

   Definition: Parenting is the chosen style, method, and technique utilized by fathers and mothers in raising (taking care of and supporting) their children.

   Challenges/Issues: Parents are role models for their children — good or bad. Children imitate their parents. Parents teach their children about life and relationships by what they do rather than what they say. Life skills to manage life as an adult are taught at home. Bad parenting is often the root of most of the problems found in modern society.

   4Tucson Goal: Every Tucson child being raised or significantly supported by a healthy father and mother.

3. **Education**

   Definition: Education is the transference of knowledge, skills, and habits from one person or group to another person, group or generation.

   Challenges/Issues: Schools must equip students with skills in reading, writing, math, sciences, history, and the arts. Students, upon graduation, should possess the ability to think critically and demonstrate the private disciplines and habits for personal success. Often genuine empathy and concern for students, their family's circumstances and socio-economic status decreases the educational process of students depriving them of the skills needed to succeed in life.

   4Tucson Goal: Become a community that values education, with Tucson area schools consistently ranking in the top 10% of schools in the country.

4. **Health and Healthcare**

   Definition: Health is the general condition of a person's body, mind, and spirit Healthcare is the diagnosis, treatment, and prevention of illness.

Challenges/Issues: Health disparities are the variations that occur in a community between different groups because of individual predispositions and personal behavioral choices. Quality of life is directly proportional to one's desire to take personal responsibility to mitigate negative predispositions (things we are born with) and to make positive individual choices (drugs, alcohol, sex outside of marriage, etc). Access to healthcare and understanding of the healthcare system makes it more easily available and affordable to those in need regardless of ethnicity, age, or socio-economic factors.

4Tucson Goal: Become a community where Tucson citizens take personal responsibility for their health and where affordable healthcare delivery systems are innovative, inventive, patient centric, and the best in the world.

5. Poverty Reduction
Definition: Poverty reduction is the process utilized to identify the root causes of poverty and to promote community environments where individuals are able to lift themselves out of poverty.

Challenges/Issues: According to the official measure from the US Census Bureau, Tucson's poverty rate as of 2012 was the eighth highest among large metropolitan statistical areas (MSAs) in the United States. Poverty in Tucson is highest among women, children, female-headed households where no husband is present, individuals living in nonfamily households, Native Americans, Hispanics, those with less than a high school degree, the foreign-born, and persons who aren't employed or who work less than full-time year-round. Of the census tracts that are fully or mostly within the City of Tucson, 15 had poverty rates above 40% between 2008 and 2012. There is a clustering with one at the northeastern city limits, one to the east, three in the south, and the remaining ten neighborhoods contiguously spanning downtown, the university area, and north of the university up Miracle Mile. One quarter of Tucson's poor live in these neighborhoods characterized by concentrated poverty.

4Tucson Goal: Tucson residents successfully: 1) graduating high school, 2) securing employment, and 3) waiting to have children until after marriage.

6. **Housing**

   Definition: Housing is the process of providing opportunities for renting or purchasing temporary or long-term shelter for individuals and/or families.

   Challenges/Issues: The self-sufficiency standard for affordability is defined at 45% or less of household income. The available supply of housing that can be purchased at the self-sufficiency standard is a critical factor in maintaining neighborhood stability. Factors that promote neighborhood stability are home ownership rate and investment into property by owners. Factors that undermine neighborhood stability are property abandonment, foreclosures, and concentration of poverty and area crime.

   4Tucson Goal: The availability of clean, safe, and affordable housing for every income level of Tucson demographic groups.

7. **Family Legacy**

   Definition: Family legacy is the process of families handing down from one generation to the next beliefs, morals, values, worldview, history, culture, traditions, opportunities, money, homes, cars, heirlooms, gifts, etc. **Challenges/issues:** God designed the family unit to provide a healthy environment to train the next generation. Tucson parents are intentional about passing on to their children many aspects of family culture including education, athletics, the arts, the family business, spiritual belief, and learning to serve others. Parents can further assist their children by building a foundation for their children and grandchildren to prosper in Tucson.

4Tucson Goal: Multi-generational families residing in Tucson.

8. **Quality of Life**

   Definition: Quality of life is the outcome of a person or groups' level of satisfaction with the environment in which they live; specifically the spiritual, social, cultural, intellectual, economic, and natural conditions.

   Challenges/Issues: Quality of life must differentiate between the subjective and objective quality of life. Subjective quality of life is about feeling good about Tucson and being satisfied with things in general and is immeasurable. Objective quality of life may be measured by several factors including: income, quality and availability of employment, class disparity, poverty rate, quality and affordability of housing, hours of work required to purchase necessities, gross domestic product (GDP), inflation rate, number of paid vacation days per year, affordable access to quality health care, quality and availability of education, life expectancy, incidence of disease, cost of goods and services, infrastructure, economic and political stability, political and religious freedom, environmental quality, climate and safety.

   4Tucson Goal: The Tucson community being a great place to raise a family.

9. **Fun Place to Live**

   Definition: A fun place to live is an environment that promotes informality, amusement, enjoyment, laughter, playfulness, and games; especially in a social and recreational context.

Challenges/Issues: The benefits of making Tucson a fun place to live would be similar to those for tourism. It brings communities together, instills a sense of pride in the community and supports local businesses. Clean, fun activities encourage families to do things together. City-wide events and festivals such as Independence Day, Christmas, Thanksgiving, Easter, and Rodeo serve to commemorate or celebrate what a community collectively values and believes is important.

4Tucson Goal: A community that promotes a wide variety of recreational/social opportunities.

City Infrastructure

City Infrastructure is the set of interconnected structural elements that provide the framework for enabling, sustaining or enhancing societal living conditions. A city's infrastructure can allow for greater efficiency in accessing the goods, services, and facilities necessary for an economy to properly function and meet the needs of its citizens.

1. **Water**

    Definition: Potable and non-potable water is essential to maintain human, animal, and plant life. Assured and Adequate Water Supply Programs are based on demonstration of a 100-year water supply considering current and committed demand, as well as growth projections.

    Challenges/Issues: It is expected that Pima County will exceed 2 million people within the next 20 years. Access to clean potable water is a primary building block for a healthy, prosperous community. It is essential to use our water resources to serve the needs of our citizens rather than dominate or manipulate their behavior. Proper management would include developing all available water resources, protecting existing water resources from contamination, maintaining and repairing of existing water delivery systems, and using various methods of conservation and reclamation.

4Tucson Goal: Assure that Tucson has a 100-year water source for two million people.

2. **Energy**
Definition: Energy is the capacity of a body or physical system to perform work. Energy is finite and no activity is possible without energy and is usually expressed in joules or kilowatt hours.

Challenges/Issues: Inexpensive, available energy is critical for the sustainability and economic prosperity of our city. Inexpensive available energy provides opportunities for upward mobility, independence ,and self-determination for people and businesses at all levels of socio-economic scale.

4Tucson Goal: Become energy independent and an energy exporter to other states.

3. **Transportation**
Definition: Transportation is the means or system by which people, goods, products, materials, and services are moved from one place to another.

Challenges/Issues: Transportation infrastructure is a critical ingredient in economic development at all levels of income. It supports personal well-being and economic growth. Transportation infrastructure plays a role as a capital input into production and wealth generation. Success of businesses is more and more tied to the speed in which a company's products can me be moved from creation to the end user. The economic impact of good transportation infrastructure can be transformative, especially at lower levels of income.

4Tucson Goal: Become a transportation hub for the movement of interstate and intrastate goods and services.

4. **Access to Capital**
   Definition: Access to capital is an environment where credit is accessible and priced appropriately to allow entrepreneurs the opportunity to start, grow, and expand business and to create jobs.

   Challenges/Issues: Small businesses employ more than half of the private sector workforce. New job creation from small businesses should be the backbone of our city's economy and the heart of our city's future. Access to capital has been and continues to be a key impediment to growth of current businesses and the start-up of new businesses.

   4Tucson Goal: To become one of the top tier financial centers in the southwest where Tucsonans of every demographic have the opportunity to access capital.

5. **Economic Opportunity and Development**
   Definition: Economic development is the sustained, concerted actions of policy makers and communities that promote the standard of living and economic health of a specific area. Economic Opportunity is the accessibility of an individual to directly participate in elevating his/her standard of living.

   Challenge/Issues: Whereas economic development is a policy intervention effort with aims of economic and social well-being of people, economic opportunity is the occurrence of individual contributions to market productivity.

4Tucson Goal: Viably tangible opportunities for upward mobility supported by public policy.

6. **Natural Resource Management**
   Definition: Natural resource management is the implementation of effective policies for the management of natural resources such as land, water, soil, plants and animals, with a particular focus on how management of each affects the quality of life for both present and future generations (stewardship).

   Challenges/Issues: Natural resource management recognizes that people and their livelihoods rely on the health and productivity of our natural resources and their actions as stewards of the land play a critical role in maintaining this health and productivity. Environmental resource management is the management of the interaction and impact of human societies on the environment. Stewardship is the high value placed on responsible planning and management of all our community resources for the benefit of its citizens.

   4Tucson Goal: To manage the resources of Tucson for the highest and best use of people.

7. **Land Use**
   Definition: Land use is the scientific, aesthetic, and orderly disposition of land, resources, facilities and services with a view to securing the physical, economic and social efficiency, health and well-being of urban and rural communities.

   Challenges/Issues: Arizona covers 72.6 million acres and is the 6th largest state (after Alaska, Texas, California, Montana and New Mexico). Land for future growth ought to be abundant, however approximately 12% of the state lands are in private hands. More land in private hands would expand the tax base and provide for more orderly growth around Arizona's largest cities.

- Federally owned 53,900,000 acres 74%
- State owned 9,800,000 acres 14%
- Privately owned 8,800,000 acres 12%

4Tucson Goal: To preserve private property rights and to encourage the conversion of 25% of publicly owned land into private ownership and expand the tax base.

CONTACT INFORMATION

Mark Harris

5151 E Broadway, Suite 1600

Tucson, AZ 85711

mark@4Tucson.com

520-745-4404

Our 4Tucson staff have prayed for God to use what we have learned to help other cities and city leaders who are interested in implementing a similar City Transformation strategy. We hope you will learn from us. We believe the contents of this book will cut your learning curve considerably.

Through the process of creating the 4Tucson model, we have developed a credible amount of expertise that may help you and your city team. We have proficiency in the following areas:

- Spiritual preparation for City Transformation.
- Developing your city team.
- Identifying and prioritizing your city's problems.
- Creating a city vision and mission.
- Developing a city model that fits your city context.
- Developing prayer as a critical part of your strategy.
- Recruiting high capacity leaders.
- Developing the internal processes to grow your city organization.
- Developing objectives, strategies, and tactics to solve city problems.
- Developing fundraising models that work.
- Staff development and evaluation processes.

- How to work through conflict.
- Overcoming obstacles that block your progress.
- The importance of becoming the neutral convener in your city.
- How to set up a Board of Directors that supports your city vision.
- School/Church Partnership Training
- Pastor Prayer Summits
- John 17 Unity Retreats
- Government/Church Partnerships

We are praying for God to bless your City Transformation efforts beyond your wildest dreams. We would be happy to come along side you to help with your city movement. Partnering together, we have the highest probability for changing, not just your city, but the world in our generation. For His glory!